Advance Praise for
Kids and Money:
Giving Them the Savvy to Succeed Financially
by Jayne A. Pearl

"Teach your kids the right money values and give them the priceless asset of financial independence. Jayne Pearl's *Kids and Money* **is a superb tool to begin the process.**"

Steve Forbes, President & Editor-in-Chief, Forbes *magazine*
President & CEO, Forbes Inc.

"... *Kids and Money* is **a must read for parents who seriously want to prepare their kids for a competitive future.**"

Jonathan Carson, Cofounder & President, Family Education Network

"Jayne Pearl's *Kids and Money* hits the nail right on the head. **This is a great resource for parents and educators alike.** In fact, we like it enough to offer it in the lobby of our bank—the world's only bank just for youth."

Linda Childears, President, Young Americans Bank

"In her book *Kids and Money,* Jayne Pearl draws on her own experience and that of experts and everyday people to help educate parents on how to properly set the course to financial success for their children. Pearl covers a wide range of topics from allowance to paying for college. *Kids and Money* **is a terrific reference for parents with kids of all ages.**"

David P. Brady, CFA, Senior Vice President & Portfolio Manager
Stein Roe & Farnham, Chicago, Illinois

KIDS *and*

MONEY

Also available from
Bloomberg Press

Investing in REITs:
Real Estate Investment Trusts
by Ralph L. Block

Smart Questions to Ask Your Financial Advisers
by Lynn Brenner

Staying Wealthy:
Strategies for Protecting Your Assets
by Brian H. Breuel

Investing in Small-Cap Stocks
by Christopher Graja and Elizabeth Ungar, Ph.D.

Investing in Hedge Funds
by Joseph G. Nicholas
(January 1999)

The New Commonsense Guide to Mutual Funds
by Mary Rowland

The Inheritor's Handbook:
A Definitive Guide for Beneficiaries
by Dan Rottenberg

A Commonsense Guide to Your 401(k)
by Mary Rowland

Bloomberg Personal Bookshelf

KIDS *and*
MONEY

Giving Them the Savvy
to Succeed Financially

JAYNE A. PEARL

BLOOMBERG PRESS

Princeton

Books are available for bulk purchases at special discounts. Special editions or book excerpts can also be created to specifications. For information, please write: Special Markets Department, Bloomberg Press.

BLOOMBERG, BLOOMBERG NEWS, BLOOMBERG FINANCIAL MARKETS, OPEN BLOOMBERG, BLOOMBERG PERSONAL FINANCE, THE BLOOMBERG FORUM, COMPANY CONNECTION, COMPANY CONNEX, BLOOMBERG PRESS, BLOOMBERG PROFESSIONAL LIBRARY, BLOOMBERG PERSONAL BOOKSHELF, and BLOOMBERG SMALL BUSINESS are trademarks and service marks of Bloomberg L.P. All rights reserved.

This publication contains the author's opinions and is designed to provide accurate and authoritative information. It is sold with the understanding that the author, publisher, and Bloomberg L.P. are not engaged in rendering legal, accounting, investment-planning, or other professional advice. The reader should seek the services of a qualified professional for such advice; the author, publisher, and Bloomberg L.P. cannot be held responsible for any loss incurred as a result of specific investments or planning decisions made by the reader.

First paperback edition published 1999
1 3 5 7 9 10 8 6 4 2

Pearl, Jayne A., 1954-
  Kids and money: giving them the savvy to succeed financially / by Jayne A. Pearl.
      p.   cm. -- (Bloomberg personal bookshelf)
  Includes index.
  ISBN 1-57660-064-5
  1. Children -- Finance, Personal.   I. Title.
  HG179.P3615   1999
  332.024'054 -- dc21   98-35789
                                                              CIP

Acquired and edited by Jared Kieling

Book design by Richard Oriolo

Permissions credits on page 239

To my parents, Buddy and Shirley Pearl,
who planted and nourished solid roots
and
To my son, Ryan, who is just beginning
to exercise his wings.

Contents

Acknowledgments

RESEARCHING AND WRITING this book enabled me to expand my knowledge of personal finance more than any previous reporting I've done over the last 18 years. It forced me to more deeply explore my attitudes and values about money. It also exposed—and helped me begin to close—gaps between what I learned and how I teach my son. If this book helps others do the same, then I and they have many folks to thank. This project emerged from the efforts and enthusiasm of several people who offered their expertise, guidance, patience, and uncommon sense. Several experts, most notably Kenneth Kaye and Robert Ortalda, who are quoted throughout, contributed valuable time and research.

All the parents I interviewed in person, by phone, or on-line are the real experts, whose insights and family trials and triumphs most guided this book. Among them I am especially indebted to Roger Ammann, Craig Aronoff, Pastor Dan Biles, Cheryl Block, Michael Brown, Joan Cramer, Fran Ferry, Shel Horowitz, Janet Isenberg, Marc Isenberg, Jon Kargman, Seth Pearl, Barbara Perman, Cecil Pollen, Joan Robb, Terry Rooney, and John Ward.

Special thanks go to Jared Kieling, my editor at Bloomberg Press, whose regular reality checks and lofty expectations pushed me to dig deeper and reach higher. Priscilla Treadwell offered many creative insights and an ample supply of cheerleading. Editorial assistants Christina Palumbo and Melissa Hafner jumped through hoops to make logistics and other details happen. Thanks, also, to the many people who worked under impossible deadlines: Barbara Diez, Mindy Weinberg, Lisa Goetz, John Crutcher,

Michelle Roth, Jacqueline Murphy, and Jack Flynn. Steven Gittelson, executive editor at *Bloomberg Personal Finance* magazine, is responsible for connecting me to Bloomberg. Jack Handler at the National Writers Union went above and beyond the call of duty with advice and support. Hillary Wonderlick, my research intern, cheerfully worked for hours tracking down arcane facts, stress-testing Web sites, and generally helping to transform chaos into order. Chelsea Pollen also astutely reviewed many Web sites from a teenager's perspective.

My sisters, Robin Kargman and Ellen Pollen, who also happen to be among my closest friends and confidants, are always there to offer sometimes painfully honest feedback, gentle nudges, and endless love. Now the ultimate pleasure is watching and helping Chelsea, Ryan, Brooke, and Tyler grow up financially and otherwise responsible, happy, and healthy.

Bruce Steinberg provided much-needed distraction whether he intended to or not, along with professional guidance and support.

Deb Ziegler at Yes Computers kept my klunker of a computer running, most of the time.

Arlene Wolf taught me the sanctity of deadlines and how to meet them—at the risk of becoming claustrophobic.

Introduction

"There are two lasting bequests we can give our children. One is roots. The other is wings."

—Hodding Carter Jr.

PARENTS WORK HARD AND WISH FOR THEIR CHILDREN to grow into physically and emotionally healthy adults. We generally do an adequate job nurturing them physically. Less often do we understand, let alone meet, their ever-evolving emotional needs. Even more rarely do we consciously consider how to help them develop into financially healthy young adults.

Today's kids will need all the help they can get to thrive financially in this world, which has changed a great deal since today's youngest parents learned what they (think they) know about money. When you were growing up, economic literacy consisted of earning, saving, and spending. Today you need to know how to save at work with 401(k)s, for example, and how to work at saving. You face complex choices about personal investments, refinancing what you buy, handling dangerously easy credit, and understanding the tax consequences of every economic move you make. Today, money management is important for just about anyone who works, not just the wealthy, and there are about a dozen personal finance magazines clamoring to help you, compared with 20 years ago when *Money* was about the only one.

Consider typical choices consumers confront day to day: 10-cents-a-minute long-distance phone plans versus rebated minutes; surcharges for ATMs versus surcharges for human tellers; leasing versus buying; Quicken versus Microsoft Money; TurboTax versus TaxCut; owning versus renting; condos versus co-ops; and tax-deferred variable annuities versus Roth IRAs. We have frequent-flier miles for credit cards and phone service; Internet banking; phone cards, fare cards, debit cards, and secured cards. Not all of these options existed 15 or even 5 years ago.

Kids don't learn the financial facts of life from their school teachers. They do absorb, from various media and friends, lots of messages, values, and attitudes—many of which you may vehemently disagree with. Where else can they turn to acquire a balanced view of the material world and to learn the basic information they will need to get by in this complex economy?

Even parents who are successful and sophisticated when it comes to personal finance tend to overlook the importance of instilling their know-how and values in this arena. Parents who are less money-savvy are more unlikely still to focus on a topic in which they lack knowledge and confidence.

Wherever you are on the spectrum of financial sophistication, it is no small task to figure out how to apply the lessons your parents and your life experiences have taught you about money to your children's high-speed, high-tech world. How can they preserve or adapt healthy financial values in the shifting sands of the global economy? After interviewing dozens of parents for this book, I have found that most have better insights and instincts than they think. What they need most are tools and techniques for applying those insights and instincts. It's one thing to decide it's time to give Sally an allowance. But how do you decide how much to give her, and how much control you should exert over how much she saves and how much she spends? Once Timmy's piggy bank is filled to the brim, what are some age-appropriate savings vehicles to help him make his money—and appreciation for saving—grow? How can you teach kids to see through society's acquisitive values? How can you hope to raise sophisticated consumers—not just in their taste for more and more material trappings, but in their ability to see through fast-paced ads that play on their fears and insecurities?

Financial child rearing requires more than footing the bills for diapers and day care, braces and bassoon lessons, summer camp and college tuition. This book will show you how to give your kids *roots*: by teaching them solid financial literacy, sound financial values, and a positive work ethic. I will also help you give your children *wings*: the savvy, confidence, and sense of independence they need to handle wisely the money they are destined to earn, invest, and eventually inherit.

Many of us are lacking in one or more of these areas ourselves. As a nation, we are poor savers, overextended borrowers, and lax budgeters. Caught in the triple squeeze of providing our kids' college tuitions, our own retirement, and our aging parents' needs, we give scant thought to helping our children develop those skills we and they need to lead more productive, successful, and secure lives.

This book will help you provide your children with a strong financial foundation from their earliest years through adulthood:

■ Television commercials bombard our kids from toddlerhood, whetting their appetite for many material things they don't need. What they do need is an understanding of the value of the dollar. This book will offer specific techniques for helping kids differentiate between needs and wants. It will suggest opportunities to work and save for the things they want.

■ Tying allowance to chores and setting guidelines for saving and spending can teach children that money doesn't come easily. But attaching such strings can also backfire, making kids resist helping out for free and possibly even creating power struggles ("It's my money, I earned it!"). This book will outline ways to maximize the positive effects of allowance, chores, and money management.

■ Credit-card companies target college and college-bound teens with enticing offers for easy credit. Given peer pressure for designer clothes and accessories (even the grunge look costs big bucks) and most teens' limited income, plastic can have drastic consequences. But are all credit cards bad or can they be useful teaching tools? This book will help parents guide their children to make responsible choices, analyze the offers, and live within their means.

■ Financial stress is the hands-down leading cause of divorce and one of the top causes of depression. This book will help parents teach kids to be practical, responsible, and confident with money and to prepare for unforeseen financial crises—lifelong skills that can avert or minimize future financial stress.

■ Fidelity Investments' High Net Worth Group says the number of U.S. millionaires will more than triple to 7.8 million in the next 20 years. Grown children who suddenly inherit large sums are often ill-equipped to make smart investment and lifestyle decisions. This book will offer techniques parents can use to instill in their children a strong work ethic and investment savvy.

To the extent you can help your children grow into responsible and skillful money earners, savers, investors, managers, and charitable givers, you enable them to lead more financially independent, productive, and happier lives.

PART I

Planting Financial Roots

Tools for grounding kids

with financial savvy, constructive

financial habits, and positive

financial values

Chapter 1

Making the Most of

Allowance, Gifts,

and Work

WHERE DOES MONEY COME FROM? THIS CAN BE AS touchy and tough a question for parents to explain to children as where babies come from. Much like sex, money is a complex issue, affected by our own childhood experiences and adult quirks and values. Unlike sex, though, the best way to teach our kids about the financial facts of life is to encourage them to begin experiencing it at an early age.

In order to experience how to deal with money, kids need to have some. There are five primary ways kids can get their little fingers on money: the dole, gifts, allowance, loans, and jobs.

This chapter will present many approaches you can

take to provide your children with "learning capital": how to develop rules based on your family's values and financial circumstances, and how to get kids thinking and learning about making trade-offs, setting goals and priorities, delaying gratification, and seeing the value of hard work. By enabling your kids to experience handling their own money and to make their own decisions and mistakes, you will give them a measurable advantage in their future financial and material success.

On the Dole

BEFORE THE TOOTH FAIRY comes for her first visit, before kids even begin to receive allowance, their first encounter with dead presidents often comes from money handed out on an as-needed, somewhat arbitrary basis.

There are some advantages to the dole system, says Prof. Sharon M. Danes, of the University of Minnesota's Department of Family Social Science. She lists several in her article, "Allowances and Alternatives," published by the Minnesota Extension Service in 1993, including:

■ More control over the kinds and amounts of children's purchases

■ Flexibility when there is irregular income

■ Works well for regular, required expenses such as school fees

■ Helps introduce the concept of money to the very young

But I'm not a big fan of this haphazard system. Parents may like the control it gives them, but the more control parents have, the less chance kids will have to learn how to handle money. Danes, who has spent a dozen years researching, training professionals, and presenting workshops to parents on family economics, points out other problems with the dole:

- May lead children to believe there's an inexhaustible supply of cash
  - Can lead to power struggles
  - Parents can lose track of how much they give to their children (which is often more than what they would give if they gave allowance)
  - Children may become better at manipulating parents than managing money
  - Children may equate purchases with love and approval

Danes suggests keeping track of how much money you give your child in a typical week and how it is spent. Make a chart with three columns: date, purpose, and amount given. After a week, use the chart to discuss with your spouse and child whether to switch to an allowance, and to base that amount on what has been spent on the dole system.

Whose Gift Is It Anyway?

ANOTHER WAY KIDS get money is when grandma or Uncle Jonathan sends a check for Brooke's birthday or a holiday. You can't control how much your kids get, but especially when they are young, you can—and should—limit how much of it they can spend and how much goes into their savings account.

Consider basing the amount of cash gifts kids can spend on their age, suggests Janet "Dr. Tightwad" Bodnar in her book, *Mom, Can I Have That?* (Kiplinger Books, 1996). For instance, preschoolers might be allowed to spend up to $20 of a cash gift—enough to buy a Barbie doll or action toy. "Six- to 12-year-olds, with more expensive tastes and a better-developed sense of how much things cost, get to spend gifts of up to $50." Bodnar recommends letting teens have discretion over gifts of up to $100.

Making Allowances

G IVING AN ALLOWANCE may seem like an easy, foolproof proposition. Allowance is an effective way to start transmitting to your kids financial literacy, values, and decision-making skills. But your decisions about timing, amount, conditions, and coordination with a spouse or ex-spouse can turn your best efforts to teach children about money into a political minefield. Fortunately, parents and other experts have staked out some safe paths through the confusion.

When to Start

The main indicators of when your child may be ready for allowance are her emotional maturity, cognitive level, and what you want allowance to accomplish. Your child will provide you with plenty of clues. You will know they're able to learn something from allowance when they:

- Become aware of the relationship between money and shopping (which generally begins at about age 3)
- Can differentiate between different coins
- Are able to count, add, and subtract
- Have opportunities for spending
- Begin asking you to buy them stuff when you shop

Don't confuse a child's interest in money with his readiness to appreciate its value. The jingle of shiny coins can be very appealing to youngsters well before they may be ready to learn about saving and spending. "I have a 5-year-old boy who loves collecting money but has no concept of its value," notes Sharon Jelinsky of Berkeley, California. "He doesn't get a regular allowance, but oftentimes he will ask if he can have the change in my pocket or at the register. He just loves collecting things."

Carol Seefeldt, professor of human development at the University of Maryland's Institute for Child Study, adds, "By around 7 or 8, depending on the child, allowance is probably necessary to teach children the meaning of money, how to use it, and how to plan." If your kids are older—even in their teens—and you haven't got them on allowance, don't worry; it's never too late to start.

Some families avoid allowance completely. "My husband and I don't believe in paying allowance on a weekly basis," says Jennifer Gerald, a stay-at-home mom in Goose Creek, South Carolina. "We are a family of six, and try to keep the 'team' mentality. We generally buy the little things (and of course the necessities) they want and need. I am wondering, though, if they will have very good money management skills as a result of what we are doing."

If you don't believe in allowances, you can give your kids other opportunities to earn cash and learn how to manage money. (Suggestions on how to do that appear later in this chapter.)

Two games can help your family put allowance in perspective:

The Allowance Game (Lakeshore Learning Materials, $14.95 plus $3.50 shipping and handling, 800-421-5354). This is even easy for young children to understand and appreciate. As they make a circuit of the board, players are instructed to do things "that kids really do," notes an 11-year-old, such as play a video game or forget their homework (and lose a turn). The first to save $20 wins.

Payday (ages 8 and up, Parker Brothers, $19.95) is a game of family finances that helps players learn about where money goes (especially unexpected dentist and house repair bills), taking out loans with interest, and taking investment risks. Players move their pieces from square to square of a one-month calendar for a predetermined number of months, have opportunities to invest in business ventures and gamble, and assume financial responsibility for day-to-day living expenses.

TABLE 1.1

Pros and Cons of Giving an Allowance

ADVANTAGES

- Promotes a sense of responsibility by teaching the value of money

- Teaches basic money management through the practice of living on a regular income

- Teaches children how to make money-related decisions and learn from mistakes

- Forces parents to define what kinds of expenses belong to children and how family values affect spending

DISADVANTAGES

- Difficult to determine the appropriate amount of money

- Can become a power issue if used as reward and punishment

- Parents may disagree about whether allowances should be earned

- If linked with household chores, children may learn that money is the only incentive for certain tasks

Source: Sharon M. Danes, Ph.D., associate professor, Minnesota Extension Service, University of Minnesota

How Much

Zillions magazine, the *Consumer Reports* for kids, polled 784 children in 1996 from age 9 to 14 and found that 46 percent received some allowance (an equal number of boys and girls; kids 13 and older were less likely to get allowance than those 12 and under). The median take was $3.50 for kids ages 9 to 10 (up 50 cents since 1994) and $5 for 11- to 14-year-olds (unchanged since 1991). Boys and girls received the same amounts.

Some experts recommend giving $1 for each year of

their age. "I personally think $5 a week is too much for a 5-year-old and that $15 is probably not enough for a 15-year-old," says Washington, D.C.–based money psychologist Olivia Mellan. What's right for your kids depends on three factors:

1. *What you expect them to pay for.* Does allowance have to cover school lunch? Movies? Clothes? If so, they'll need more than kids who brown-bag it to school and whose parents cover regular living expenses.

2. *The child's level of maturity.*

3. *What you can afford.* Not everyone can afford to pay their kids (especially if the family is large) several dollars a week. That can be a lesson itself. In an interview, Danes explained, "When parents include children in discussions of family financial problems, they are quite often surprised at how supportive and helpful children can be during these times. However, my research shows if you don't sit down in times of difficulty and talk to children about what's going on, they will assume they have done something wrong and that they are at fault."

Negotiating Raises

Eventually, many kids feel they need more money. They may just be getting greedy, they may feel the need for more financial independence, or they may find it difficult to pay for a growing list of expenses you expect them to cover. The *Zillions* survey found that almost 4 out of 10 kids who receive allowance get a raise automatically every year, although two out of every three children who asked for a raise didn't get one. Danes insists that allowance does not need to automatically increase each year. She says there are two reasons for a raise: escalating costs of expenses the child covers, such as school lunch; or you expect allowance to cover more expenses as the child matures. "That gets at the issue of having a reason for giving allowance," explains Danes. "There's no lesson to teach when the children expect an increase just because they're a year older. Instead, the reason for getting a greater part of the family income pie is so they can learn more about balancing demands and resources. It's a good time to review with them what they're getting, how they're spending it, setting priorities, and decision-making."

Instead of dismissing their requests (or demands) and snapping shut your wallet, open up the lines of communication. Ginger Ogle, a software writer, has two sons, 11 and 14. When they complained a couple years ago that they were not getting enough and claimed that everyone was getting more allowance than they were, she suggested they survey their friends. "It was enlightening for them," says Ogle, who also moderates the University of California at Berkeley Parents Network, an e-mail list of more than 600 parents associated with UCB who share information. "They found out that most of their friends were getting either the same or *less* than they were getting."

But be careful not to focus only on what other kids are getting. Patrick Ellis, another member of the UCB Parents Network, warns, "At least one of my kids always seems to have a close friend from a fairly wealthy family, so I avoid this tactic. When I tried it with my eldest when he was 6 it turned out he had a friend who got $50 a month—with no savings requirement."

Remember, allowance is supposed to be a teaching tool. Negotiation skills are an important part of that, which they're going to need for dealing effectively with friends, teachers, and eventually, their boss. Going rates in the marketplace are only one factor you might use when lobbying for a raise with your boss. Another key consideration is cost-of-living increases. Tell kids itching for a raise to document increases in the things they pay for. You can also tell them to list new expenses they might be willing to cover after an allowance hike. If you pay for school lunches now, you can add that amount to their current allowance, giving them the option of making their own lunch so they have more discretionary income. One mother did that with her 12- and 16-year-old daughters. The only problem she reports is, "The older one will skip eating to save money."

It may be fun and enlightening for you and your child to compare what their allowance would have been when you were their age. You can do just that with *Exercise 1.1*.

EXERCISE 1.1:

Allowance—Then and Now

To calculate what your child's allowance (or the price of anything) today was worth when you were their age, follow these three easy steps:

1. Determine the year you were the child's age:

Your birth year + child's age =   _____

2. Fill in the Consumer Price Index from the chart on the following page for the above year:

CPI the year you were the child's

current age =   _____

3. Calculate the value of your child's allowance when you were the child's current age:

Child's allowance × CPI when

you were their age (#2 above)

÷ CPI this year   =   _____

For example, in 1998, my son, age 10, earns $4 allowance a week. I was born in 1954, so when I turned 10 in 1964, the CPI was 31.0. The CPI in 1998 is 162.2. Therefore, in 1964, his $4 a week allowance would have been worth 76 cents. In other words, 76 cents in 1964 would be equivalent to $4 today:

$$\$4 \times \frac{31}{162.2} = \$0.76$$

Year	Consumer Price Index (1982–84=100)	Year	Consumer Price Index (1982–84=100)
1945	18.0	1972	41.8
1946	19.5	1973	44.4
1947	22.3	1974	49.3
1948	24.1	1975	53.8
1949	23.8	1976	56.9
1950	24.1	1977	60.6
1951	26.0	1978	65.2
1952	26.5	1979	72.6
1953	26.7	1980	82.4
1954	26.9	1981	90.9
1955	26.8	1982	96.5
1956	27.2	1983	99.6
1957	28.1	1984	103.9
1958	28.9	1985	107.6
1959	29.1	1986	109.6
1960	29.6	1987	113.6
1961	29.9	1988	118.3
1962	30.2	1989	124.0
1963	30.6	1990	130.7
1964	31.0	1991	136.2
1965	31.5	1992	140.3
1966	32.4	1993	144.5
1967	33.4	1994	148.2
1968	34.8	1995	152.4
1969	36.7	1996	156.9
1970	38.8	1997	160.5
1971	40.5	1998*	162.2

*Average through May

Source: Bureau of Labor Statistics

Looked at backward, if I had received $4 a week in 1964, it would be worth $20.93 today:

$$\$4 \times \frac{162.2}{31} = \$20.93$$

Here's another fun way to look at it. When I was a kid, I used to get five cents for each year of my age. When I was 10, I got 50 cents a week. In today's dollars, that would be worth only $2.62:

$$\$0.50 \times \frac{162.2}{31} = \$2.62$$

Coordination with Spouses, Ex-Spouses, and Blended Families

Two things contribute to making allowance an effective learning tool: consistency and coordination between parents.

For consistency, give whatever amount you chose at a set time. The most popular pay period is once a week, but every other week is fine. One mother says her 7½-year-old son prefers to get paid monthly. The longer the interval, the more they will have to learn how to plan and budget.

Coordination can be harder to achieve, because each parent may have different attitudes about money. "How money was handled in your family when you were a child affects how you handle money with your children," says Danes. "And because often opposites attract, couples can have conflicting attitudes about money, which can erupt when topics such as allowance come up." For instance, one parent may come from a family in which money was never discussed in front of children or in any public arena. Her partner's family of origin may have been perfectly comfortable discussing family finances. Put them together and complex issues can arise.

"It means a lot more discussion has to go on about how you bring those two ends of the continuum together and create a united front when you address those issues with children," says Danes. "As long as you work it out, you can even have the children hear you talk about things and watch you come to compromises."

For starters, she suggests that parents sit down and share their answers to the following questions:

- What does money mean to you?
- What memories, good and bad, about money do you have from your childhood?
- If you got allowance, what were the rules about it?
- If you didn't get allowance, how did you receive or obtain money?
- What attitudes or feelings about money have you carried into adulthood based on your family's approach to money when you were a child?
- Which of your attitudes about money would you like to instill in your children?

It's crucial for parents in an intact family to make rules as a team, says Skokie, Illinois–based family therapist and psychologist Kenneth Kaye, Ph.D., who specializes in working with family businesses. In his insightful and pragmatic book, *Family Rules: Raising Responsible Children Without Yelling or Nagging* (St. Martin's Paperbacks, 1984), Kaye says, "It is almost impossible for a mother to enforce a set of rules if the children's father lives in the home but has no part in creating the rules or does not back up his wife when she tries to enforce them. It is equally impossible for a father to succeed with such a system without the active participation of his wife."

For divorced parents, coordination with the other parent can be harder. The good news is, coordination does not mean that the amount of allowance and rules attached to spending, saving, and chores have to be identical.

Patrick Ellis, a divorced supervisor of programmer analysts at the University of California at Berkeley, notes that he and his ex-wife have "tried to consult—or at least inform—each other about the way we do the kids' finances and chores. This is not to say that we do it identically. But it helps a lot to at least know what is going on at the other house, so if nothing else, the kids can't play you against each other, and you can try to maintain something approaching a balance when making your own decisions."

Many divorced parents have a hard time agreeing on anything or even communicating at all. Not to worry, Kaye assured me in an interview: "In a divorced family with remarriages or equivalent long-term relationships, each set of partners has to make rules autonomously for their own household." He adds, "Clearly kids can live under different sets of rules in different homes."

He describes the friend of his son whose parents are divorced and who lives with his mother and stepfather in a middle-class neighborhood. The father, who is wealthier, lives with his new wife in a big house with a swimming pool. "He can buy things for the son beyond the mom and step-dad's means. While he's not inappropriate about it, his thresholds are different and unconsciously there is probably a desire to make it up to the child for not being there when he was little. The kid lives in two different worlds."

Kaye notes, "What goes on in the other household can make ex-spouses crazy. They should concentrate on things they can control. Parents who are still playing games with each other and who are hostile have wonderful opportunities to zing each other by making offers to the child that no reasonable co-parent could object to. For example, what could be objectionable about a father giving his son a car? Well, if instead of saying, 'I have a car you can have if your mom lets you,' he does not coordinate with the co-parent before the car is offered, the car could put the child in a damned-if-he-does, damned-if-he-doesn't situation. By accepting or rejecting the gift he will get one parent or the other angry." Kaye suggests that the father call his ex-wife and her new husband first to make sure they have no problem, and to work out who will pay for gas and insurance and how to govern the use of the car.

Ellis reports, "We've eliminated all the 'but over at my Mom's/Dad's . . .' stuff, and I think we're also helping the kids to appreciate that there are different ways of doing things and no one way is necessarily the only right (or wrong) way."

What about the complexities of blended families?

Cecil, a computer consultant in Chicago, gives each of his two teens, ages 13 and 18, a $100 per month allowance. His new wife's 14-year-old daughter had always gotten about half that amount. "When we became a blended family, she demanded 'equity' from her mother and stepfather. But since the stepdaughter has a child support check coming from her father, her mother feels that her amount is in line with the support." In the name of family harmony, though, Cecil caved in. "Parity is working out okay, except that my stepdaughter never thanked anyone for it," he laments. "Ungrateful is a good word here."

Terms and Conditions

To many parents, it seems natural to tie allowance to behavior or grades. Three out of four kids in the *Zillions* survey said their parents did so, and 40 percent had some allowance withheld the month before the survey. However, many experts and parents find it is more effective to encourage good behavior or grades with praise and attention, which boost self-esteem and generate greater internal motivation.

Behavior

Dawn Davidson, another member of the University of California at Berkeley Parents Network, found that out the hard way. When her foster daughter, Victoria, was 10,

Davidson would deduct some allowance "for certain unde-sirable behaviors such as lying about whether or not she did her homework. That was only effective for a short while. One of Victoria's coping mechanisms is to make whatever is bothering her 'not matter.'" So after a while of having her allowance withheld, she would stop caring (or claim to) and continue neglecting homework. "Now we only withhold part of her allowance if whatever she did actually cost us money. For example, when she wanted the school yearbook but didn't get us the information until after the price had gone up, we made her pay for the difference out of her allowance."

But some parents insist bribery works fine for them. Dianna Bolt, a word processor at UCB, docks her 7-year-old son for "not doing, or balking at, things he is supposed to do, such as brushing his teeth in the morning or taking a bath." For instance, when he refuses to take his dishes into the kitchen after eating, Bolt deducts 10 cents from his $1 a week allowance. "Also, I've set up a thing where if I have to tell him more than three times to do something, this is 5 cents off his allowance. I don't keep to this absolutely, but do take a little off now and then for this. Usually I just have to say, 'This is the third time I'm telling you,' and he will do what he is supposed to do."

Still, many experts suggest reinforcing positive behav-ior with special outings or expressing appreciation. Using money is bound to teach your kids to put a monetary value on thoughtfulness or on their achievements.

Grades

As with behavior-based bucks, experts tend to frown on paying for good grades. "If you design a system where you're paying kids for things they ought to do for the satis-faction of doing it, you are in danger of erasing the intrinsic reward," says Kaye. "When a kid comes home with a good report card and they're proud, there's no better reward than to tell them how proud you are."

Cathy Adler, a part-time administrative assistant in New Milford, Connecticut, doesn't like the idea of paying for good grades for her 12-year-old daughter or 10-year-old son. She points out, "An *A* in an easy subject is nothing, but a *C* in a subject that's tough is wonderful. I'm more concerned with the learning, improvement, and attitude. Grades in isolation are worthless. I feel that my children should always try their best. The reward is their grade. I do take them out to dinner if I feel their grades are equal to what they can achieve."

Rhonda Weide, a single mother of three in Wilsonville, Oregon, says, "I believe giving a bonus for good grades is akin to work in 'real' life, where employees get bonuses according to company profits and employee contribution." The recently laid-off case worker for an insurance company says she pays them at midterm and the end of the semester, based on effort as well as her total budgetary restrictions. However, Weide has found that less direct monetary rewards can be more effective than cold cash: "On two occasions, my kids opted to forgo their grade bonus in lieu of a vacation to a spot I didn't think I could afford—surprisingly, their grades were the best in those two instances."

Chores

Tying allowance to chores is a double-edged sword. On the plus side, it can instill kids with a sense of responsibility and a positive work ethic. On the negative side, putting a price tag on household tasks takes away the incentive for kids to help out just for the sake of doing a good deed. The whole thing can backfire when kids decide, "I don't feel like dusting the living room. I don't care if you don't pay me." Or it can inspire little mercenaries to declare, "I'll only help you bring up the groceries if you pay me."

Parent Cathy Adler tried it both ways. But she had a hard time giving her kids an allowance when their rooms were dirty and they didn't do their chores. "I thought I wouldn't get paid if I didn't do what was expected from me on my job, so why should I pay them?" That inspired her to sit down and have a talk with her kids about how she and her husband, an engineer, earn money and what they do with it. She asked them what they need money for, and whether they felt they should be paid if they didn't do their chores. "They both agreed, no. I must admit that sometimes they don't care about the money and I live with a dirty room for a while. But when they want something, you wouldn't believe how all their chores get done. I also notice the older they get, the more they want so the more they do their chores to get money."

Paying for chores might work in the short run, but if the purpose in giving an allowance is to enable your children to practice being responsible for some of their own spending and saving, then paying them for chores may only complicate and undermine that goal. As University of Maryland Prof. Carol Seefeldt insists, "I dislike giving kids allowance for taking out garbage or making their bed, on the grounds that women don't get paid to do these things." Children (and fathers, too!) should have to contribute to household chores, just because they are part of the family. Kids should be given increasing responsibility, as they get older, for a fair share of household chores.

However, if kids want to earn extra money, there's nothing wrong with paying them to do tasks you would otherwise pay someone else to do—such as mowing the lawn, washing the car, housecleaning, or shoveling snow. You will find several creative ways to do this later in this chapter, under "Work for Pay."

Debi Dee, an Orangevale, California–based book-keeper, reports, "We sat down and listed every possible chore that needs to be done to run the house. The kids were amazed at what was involved. We split doing the dishes up on a weekly basis. Everyone has one week when they are responsible for the dishes and kitchen. This includes my

TABLE 1.2

Two-Tiered Allowance System

ALLOWANCES

	Irrevocable	+	Revocable	=	Total/Wk.)
Billy (8)	$ 0.25		0.75		= $ 1
Laurie (10)	$ 0.50		1.50		= $ 2
Bob (13)	$ 5.00		5.00		= $10
Karen (17)	$11.00		5.00		= $16

Source: *Family Rules: Raising Responsible Children Without Yelling or Nagging*, Kenneth Kaye (St. Martin's Paperbacks, 1984)

husband and myself. That week seems long, but then come four weeks when it's not your turn! The rest of the chores were divided up by going around the table and everyone picking chores. I then made a list of chores, whose turn it is, and how often the chore needs to be done. Every five weeks (because that's a complete dish rotation) we look the list over and can re-pick chores if someone is unhappy. This really seems to be working. No one complains that they have to do all the work."

In *Family Rules*, Kaye suggests a two-tiered system, in which he treats part of the allowance as irrevocable, "to be given to the child even if the other portion has to be withheld as punishment. Older children may need bus fare or lunch money every school day. (Treat it as a per diem: no school, no lunch and bus money for that day.) Everything beyond that is extra spending money." *Table 1.2, above,* illustrates how that might work for kids of different ages.

Loans and Advances

HANDING OUT ADVANCES—even with interest—is not a great idea. There are several problems:

■ It misses an opportunity to instill a tolerance for delayed gratification that is so important to creating a cycle of success.

■ "It teaches them 'buy now, pay later,'" warns family therapist Kenneth Kaye. "And by not charging a hefty interest rate, you give your child precisely the miseducation that finance companies exploit: the impression that credit is 'E-Z', as all the ads say."

■ It robs children of a sense of independence and self-esteem that comes when they work toward and achieve goals on their own.

Kaye adds that "these objections wouldn't apply in the case of an adult son or daughter for whom you might finance a car or a home on more attractive terms than they could get commercially."

There are times, such as finding something on sale that your child has been saving for, when making a loan is reasonable. On such occasions, by laying out the terms in a very businesslike manner you will create a different kind of learning opportunity. Lucinda, a creative mom, has a unique setup. To teach her children to learn about the world of finance, she created a "family bank" from which her children can borrow money. Just like a regular bank, the family bank has contracts, charges interest, asks for collateral, and even repossesses. She has repossessed roller blades, tapes, CDs, and a remote-control car. Sounds harsh? Perhaps, but she has never had to repossess from the same child twice. Better they learn by losing a $7 tape or $20 roller blades at age 13 or 14 than by losing a $10,000 car at age 25.

In general, not giving into kids' whims teaches them how to live with delayed gratification. "Not having instantaneous gratification is so important to later life," notes

University of Maryland's Carol Seefeldt. "Kids need to learn that they can work for a distant goal and that they don't have to have a reward right away. Learning to wait enables them to set a goal, make a plan, and take small steps toward achieving that goal. Kids who are not doing well in school and are at risk of dropping out have not learned the value of spending time to get the high school diploma or going to college."

Work for Pay

WHILE, IDEALLY, ALLOWANCE should not be tied to chores, you can pay kids to do tasks you might otherwise pay someone else for. Putting your little laborers to work is a great opportunity to teach them about the connection between work and money, and to help them develop a sense of pride and responsibility in being compensated for achieving a hard-earned goal.

A good rule of thumb might be to divvy up household chores among family members, without pay, for the jobs parents would normally do, and hire kids who want to earn extra cash to perform tasks you would otherwise pay an outsider to do. *Table 1.3, right,* lists types of household activities appropriate for kids at different ages.

One parent set up a card system for money-earning chores for her 14-year-old daughter and 5-year-old son. Each card has a certain chore with the amount that will be paid when it's completed. For example, $5 for bathroom cleaning, $2 for dusting top shelves, and $7.50 for organizing a closet. The card also has the specifications of how the job should be done. "We try to be as specific as possible because the kids will find a loophole, like when you tell them to clean their room and it all goes under the bed," she explains. She keeps a separate card system for each child, so they have a choice of age-appropriate jobs and earnings. Each time one of the children completes a job, he or she signs and dates the card and returns it to the card box. "At the end of the week we

TABLE 1.3

Jobs for Kids

AGE	GOTTAS—NO PAY	EXTRAS—FOR PAY
Age 5+	make bed; clear/ set table	dust; water plants; weed garden
Age 7+	(all above, plus): fold/put away clean laundry; wash dishes	(all above, plus): sweep; rake leaves; feed, walk, clean up after pet; wash windows
Age 10+	(all above, plus): clean own bathroom; take out trash	(all above, plus): wash car; vacuum house; home office tasks such as filing, collating, stamping, sealing out-going mail
Age 12+	(all above, plus): do own laundry	(all above, plus): baby-sit sibs; mow lawn; shovel snow; mop floors; clean bathrooms

check the cards, calculate what we owe, and make a check out to the 14-year-old, but usually give the 5-year-old cash."

"Our goal is to get our children to think about working first rather than asking for a loan at the last minute," says Linda, a Michigan artist and parent of Kyle, 11, and Niki, 14. "We're not quite there yet, but getting better. Slowly. At least this way they know life is not a free ride. And it must be working because I overheard my daughter turn down an invitation to the movies with a friend, saying she already owed me too much and couldn't afford to go. That's a first."

A little work never hurt anyone. Some kids over age 11 find jobs in the community such as paper routes or find meaningful volunteer work. Parents who have their own company can hire their kids.

Kids on the Family Business Payroll

Many business owners hire their kids during summers or after school to sweep, file, collate, stuff envelopes, input data, organize office supplies, or answer the phones. If you are a sole proprietor (14.9 million people, or 11.5 percent of the labor force, were self-employed in 1997), putting kids on the payroll is great for the business-owner parent. The business gets to deduct reasonable salaries paid to dependent children under age 18. Gerald Hersh, an enrolled agent in Northampton, Massachusetts, says that most sole proprietors in the top 28 percent federal tax bracket will save at least 43 cents (28 cents from the deducted salary and 15 cents from reduced self-employment taxes) in federal taxes on each dollar up to $4,250 they pay their children. There should also be a reduction in state taxes.

Children under age 18 can earn 1998 wage income up to $4,250 tax-free. Sole proprietors do not have to withhold Social Security taxes or unemployment taxes for kids under age 18 on their payroll. This does not apply to shareholders of a closely held corporation or partnership.

Hiring your kids can also be great for them—if you give them clear guidelines about what you expect of them.

Assign the right job for the right age

You need to spell out not only how many hours you expect them to work, but also what tasks you require them to complete in that time. Make sure those tasks match their skill level. "If you give them something that's over their head, they'll get frustrated and lose confidence. If you assign them tasks below their abilities, they'll get bored," warns Leslie Dashew, president of Human Side of Enterprise, a consulting firm in Atlanta.

Set reasonable work hours

Business owners who employ their own children are not restricted by the child labor law, which stipulates that children cannot begin working until age 11. However, because the federal law was designed to protect children, it is a sensible guide for setting hours. During the school year, the law says kids 11 through 15 can log in up to three hours a day between 7 a.m. and 7 p.m. during the school year and up to 9 p.m. when school's out. There are no restrictions on children 16 or older. Remember, though, that kids also need unstructured time with their peers.

Pay fair wages

Many business owners make one of two mistakes: they either overpay or underpay their kids. One rule of thumb is to pay them what you would have to pay other employees to perform similar work. "You can't pay a 15-year-old $10,000 to come in and file for a week," says Mary Jane Rynd, a partner with Rynd Carneal & Ewing, a Phoenix-based law firm. Inflated pay sets unreasonable expectations about the value of work. And of course, any amount the IRS considers to be "unreasonable compensation" is not deductible to the family business.

But here's a tricky one: Should you pay your 12-year-old computer wiz the same $20 an hour (or more) you might have to pay a professional to write a complex software program for your business? No, says money psychologist Olivia Mellan. "You should factor in a combination of their age and what feels right to them. You shouldn't pay them more than what feels like a good salary to them. Having a lot of money can feel weird, not great, to a kid."

Mellan's son, for instance, is an actor. At age 11, while on location in Los Angeles shooting a movie, the producers gave him $50 per diem for food and incidentals. "We decided my son should handle that. He couldn't believe how expensive food in L.A. is, and got quite horrified. I thought that was a great learning experience. But toward the end of the week, he was extremely exhausted and pressured. He got very teary and said, 'When we get home you're still going to support me, right?' The money and the responsibility were too much for him."

Tim Rouch pays his four children, now ages 13 to 18, $5 to $8 an hour to work on his tree farm and lawn mower/ chain saw retail and repair shop in Three Rivers, Michigan. During the school year the two older kids work three or four hours a night plus all day Saturday repairing mowers and spraying trees. The youngest boy helps out the older ones; his daughter does inventory and other farm chores when she needs money. They also have household chores, such as mowing the lawn and washing dishes, for which they do not get paid. Summers the children work about 40 hours a week.

"When they turned 8, they started paying for everything except rent and food," explains Rouch. "They pay for all their clothes, ski equipment, and lift tickets, even their own dentist bills—though we pay their doctor bills. If they want $100 tennis shoes, they know they'll have less to put toward other things."

Piece rates may evoke images of exploited immigrants or children in sweatshops, but Carolyn and Rick Crandall, owners of Select Press, a Corte Madera, California–based newsletter publishing business, found that a piece rate felt fairer to everyone in the family than paying their kids, now 20, 16, and 13, by the hour. The three children have worked since about age 5 licking stamps and folding paper, and now help collate, label, and stuff envelopes for monthly mailings. "When we paid them an hourly rate, the kids slowed down. With a piece rate they can make a very good wage if they move right along." The older kids had also resented earning the same rate as the youngest. Now, because they can work faster than their younger siblings, they can earn more.

William Hutson, owner of TSA America and Teracom, two Little Compton, Rhode Island, home-based companies that develop and license medical, communications, and physical science techniques, hired his sons when they were 13 and 17, when his business hit hard times. "We couldn't afford to pay them allowance, but it wasn't just a way to help them earn money—I needed their help." The work he hired his two sons, now 17 and 21, to perform didn't lend itself to a piece rate. Their main tasks included inputting and organizing data on the computer, conducting on-line information searches, and reviewing briefings and technical papers. Even before he officially began working for his father, the younger son designed the company's logo at age 11. They earned $5 an hour when they started a new, unfamiliar project. As they got up to speed, he paid them up to $10 to $25 an hour—the same he'd have to pay someone else.

Teach on the job

There's nothing wrong with hiring kids to answer phones, do filing, or clean the office, but it's important to explain how any tasks they perform contribute to the business.

Work experience in your business, at home, or as volunteers not only keeps kids off the street, it also can provide kids with important life lessons, such as:

- Job skills (which can help college applicants stand out from peers)
- Discipline
- Greater appreciation for the value of a hard-earned dollar
- How to get along with superiors and peers
- How to cope with a tedious routine
- Greater understanding of adults who must put up with jobs all the time

But there are some potential problems to monitor:

- *With fewer hours to do homework, watch out for slip-*

ping grades. Studies by Jerald G. Bachman and John Schulenberg of the University of Michigan's Institute for Social Research (ISR) have found that teens who work more than 20 hours per week get lower grades in school (although the authors of the research are not sure whether the work causes lower grades, or kids with low grades tend to work 20 or more hours a week).

■ *While jobs may keep kids off the street, the extra money and stress may make it easier and more tempting to buy things they might not ordinarily have the cash or inclination to buy, including drugs.* In a 1993 article in *Developmental Psychology,* Bachman and Schulenberg contend that working teens are more likely to use drugs and alcohol and are less connected to their families than teens who don't work as much. (Please see "Setting Limits on Kids' Spending" in Chapter 4 for ways to offset some of these risks.)

■ *Children today are subjected to tremendous pressure and competition.* Homework, household chores, sports, music lessons and practicing, religious school, and clubs already leave kids with precious little leisure time. "Work intensity appears to reduce the likelihood of getting sufficient sleep, eating breakfast, exercising, and having a satisfactory amount of leisure time," write Bachman and Schulenberg in their article. Make sure a job won't rob your kids of time to just veg out and relax.

"I have to remember that my kids are kids and they need the opportunity to grow up on their own terms with their own peers," says Hutson.

Kid-Preneurs

Flipping burgers or delivering newspapers may seem like the only jobs kids can find in the community, and even those can be tough to get in some regions. With some imagination and ambition, kids can do what more and more downsized grown-up employees resort to: start their own business. Not only can it be more fun and profitable, but it can also provide an excellent learning experience.

Lemonade stands, baby-sitting, lawn mowing, and newspaper routes are common "businesses" kids have undertaken. But creative and savvy kids can learn how to tap their unique talents and interests and base a business on them. Most entrepreneurs build their business around something they feel passionate about. If your child is a computer wiz, she can teach clients how to navigate the Internet, use new software programs, get their office PCs networked, or even shop for the right computer.

Fourteen-year-old Jodi, a great animal lover, started a neighborhood pet-sitting service. "I have business cards, which I make myself on my computer. I give reports to the people on how their pet was while they were gone, I give out newsletters once a month, and I advertise around my neighborhood. I get on my bike and make my rounds four times a day nonstop and make anywhere from $50 to up to $200 a week. It's very profitable—I recently got a backyard kennel put in, which is cheaper for my customers than a commercial kennel, and the animal gets more attention."

She started small—watching her friend's cat. "Then the owner of a littermate of my dog asked if I would watch her dog while she was out of town. That triggered the idea. I started making a few calls, then started advertising and doing more and more business. That led to business cards and flyers." She even has her own Web site, which describes her business services and offers tips on caring for various types of pets.

Parents can remind their kids to factor in all costs and identify where that "start-up capital" will come from (savings? a loan from parents?). Tracking financial results is an important learning exercise. Kids are often shocked when they realize that their profit is what they are left with after they subtract expenses.

TABLE 1.4

Resources for Kid-Preneurs

BOOKS

- *Better than a Lemonade Stand,* by Daryl Bernstein and Rob Huberg (Beyond Words Publishing, 1992), $9.95.
- *Fast Cash for Kids,* by Bonnie and Drew Noel (Career Press, 1995), $13.99 plus $3.50 shipping, 800-227-3371.
- *Kidbiz: Everything You Need to Start Your Own Business,* by Conn McQuinn and Mike Reddy (Penguin/Puffin Mass Market, 1998), $10.99.
- *The Kid's Business Book,* by Arlene Erlbach (Lerner Publications Company, 1998), $22.60.
- *The Lemonade Stand,* by Emmanuel Modu and James B. Hayes (Gateway Publishers, 1996), $19.95. Helps parents guide and encourage their kids' entrepreneurial urges.
- *Making Cents: Every Kid's Guide to Money,* by Elizabeth Wilkinson (Little, Brown & Co, 1989), $12.95.
- *The Monster Money Book,* by Loreen Leedy (Holiday, 1992), $14.95.
- *No More Frogs to Kiss: 99 Ways to Give Economic Power to Girls,* by Joline Godfrey (HarperCollins, 1995), $12.
- *Teen's Guide to Business: The Secrets to a Successful Enterprise,* by Rickell Fisher, Oren Jenkins, Linda Menzies, and Owen Jenkins (MasterMedia, 1992), $7.95.

GAMES

- **An Income of Her Own,** a board game for up to eight players, ages 12+, by the author of *No More Frogs to Kiss* (see above), $38 plus $8 shipping, 800-350-2978.
- **The Lemonade Stand,** by Jason Mayans (www.little-jason.com/lemonade/lemonadeb.cgi), simulates a lemonade stand on a neighbor's yard (for $0.75 a day rent). Based on a daily weather forecast, players must decide how many cups

of lemonade to make, how much to charge, and whether to advertise. For each day's play, the game calculates how many cups you sell, your expenses that day, and your profit. Free on its Web page.

■ **Gazillionaire Deluxe,** a CD–ROM business simulation of a commodities trading company in outer space, in which players make decisions about supply and demand, profit margins, and overhead, $34.99. Free shareware version and other software can be downloaded from LavaMind's Web page (www.lavamind.com/edu.html), or call 415-566-3808.

■ **Zapitalism Deluxe,** by LavaMind, a more sophisticated game than Gazillionaire that lets older kids who can understand complex math and economics start a retail business on an imaginary island and try to build it into an empire, $39.99.

■ **Profitania Deluxe,** LavaMind's most advanced business-simulation game, involves a factory in an imaginary subterranean world, $44.99.

ORGANIZATIONS

■ **An Income of Her Own.** Helps teen girls develop economic empowerment. A $20 annual membership comes with a newsletter, invitations to special events, application to the National Teen Business Plan Competition, tickets to satellite broadcasts, and conferences. 1804 West Burbank Boulevard, Burbank, CA 91506, 800-350-2978 (www.anincomeofherown.com).

■ **Busines$ Kids.** A company that helps 10- to 18-year-olds start a business (Joseph Vincent, EVP). 1 Alhambra Plaza, Suite 1400, Coral Gables, FL 33134, 305-445-8869.

■ **Do Something.** Provides training, guidance, and financing to youth. 423 West 55th Street, New York, NY 10019, 212-978-7777 or 212-523-1175.

■ **Educational Designs That Generate Excellence (EDGE).** Collaborates with schools, youth agencies, colleges, teachers, and corporations to help provide entrepreneurship education through teacher training, in/after school programs, entrepreneurship camps (please see below), curriculum, conferences, keynote presentations, and customized youth program consulting, 800-879-3343.

■ **The Entrepreneurial Development Institute.** Helps disadvantaged 7- to 21-year-olds start their own business. 2024 I Street, NW, Suite 905, Washington, DC 20006, 202-822-8334.

■ **Future Business Leaders of America.** An educational association of more than 250,000 students (who must be enrolled in at least one business class) preparing for careers in business. Has 13,000 chapters at middle schools, high schools, and colleges in the United States. 1912 Association Drive, Reston, VA 22091, 703-860-3334 (www.FBLA-PBL.org).

■ **Junior Achievement.** Volunteer-based, in-class and afterschool programs to teach K–12 students about economics, starting and running a business, and the global economy. Its 232 U.S. affiliates reach almost 3 million students a year. One Education Way, Colorado Springs, CO 80906, 719-540-8000 (www.ja.org).

■ **Young Americans Bank.** Runs Young AmeriTowne program, a hands-on program for students to run their own life-size town including various shops and businesses. Also has a free brochure, *How to Prepare a Business Plan.* 311 Steele Street, Denver, CO 80206, 303-321-2954 (www.theyoungamericans.org).

SUMMER CAMPS

■ **Biz Builders**. A two-week program held in Wellesley, Massachusetts, sponsored by the National Foundation for Teaching Entrepreneurship (NFTE). Cost: $1,550. 800-367-6383.

■ **Biz Camp.** A coed camp for low-income students, also sponsored by the NFTE. Free. 800-367-6383.

■ **Camp Entrepreneur.** A one-week program for girls ages 12 to 19 put on by the National Education Center for Women in Business. Held in Atlanta; Youngstown, Ohio; Jacksonville, Florida; Locust Valley, New York. Cost: $225 to $495. 800-632-9248.

■ **Camp $tartup.** Two-week sessions ($1,400 per session) on college campuses in San Francisco and Boston teach girls ages 13 to 18 business and leadership skills, including marketing, operations, finance, planning, research, networking, technology, negotiation, stress management, and business etiquette. Run by An Income of Her Own, 800-350-2978.

■ **Center for Teen Entrepreneurship.** P.O. Box 3967, New York, NY 10163, 973-824-7207.

■ **Kidsway Entrepreneurship Camp.** A three-day program teaches real-world business skills, team building, leadership, financial management, verbal communications skills, and business etiquette, and helps them create a business name and slogan, design business cards and flyers, develop a written business plan, and videotape a commercial to advertise their product. Cost: $495. 888-543-7929.

■ **Youth Entrepreneurship Business Camp.** One- and two-week camp for boys and girls sponsored by Educational Designs That Generate Excellence (EDGE) in New York, Boston, Houston, San Diego, and Atlanta. Every student starts their own business, designs their own set of business cards, opens a savings account, becomes a shareholder in a public company, learns to read the stock pages, sells at a trade fair, writes and presents a business plan complete with posters, flyers, videotaped commercials, and financial statements, and is recognized for their achievements at a closing awards ceremony. Cost: $500 to $1,500 (some camps for low-income children are free). 800-879-3343.

■ **Young AmeriTowne Camp.** A five-day day camp in Denver run by Young Americans Education Foundation. Students apply and interview for jobs, elect a mayor and judge, create laws, manage bank accounts, act as producers and consumers, and see the impact of their decisions on the town economy. Cost: $135. 303-321-2954.

GETTING KIDS STARTED with allowance and work, or more thoughtfully approaching the way you have been doing it, helps your children develop positive attitudes and habits about money. The next step is guiding your budding capitalists to make smart decisions about what to do with the money they amass—how to preserve it and make it grow. Chapter 2 will show you how to inspire kids to save and invest their hard-earned dollars wisely.

TABLE 1.5

Allowance and Work Tips to Remember

1. Be consistent: give kids a set amount of allowance the same time each week.

2. Coordinate with your current spouse and jointly enforce all rules concerning money, including saving, spending, loans, and chores.

3. Don't worry if an ex-spouse has different rules. Just make sure you and your current partner agree on rules and back each other up.

4. Make advances and loans the exception, not the rule.

5. When you do make a loan, set up repayment terms in a businesslike fashion.

6. Think twice before tying allowance to chores, behavior, or grades.

7. Pay a base allowance unconditionally—without tying it to "gottas" (chores they must do)—and provide a list of "extras" (jobs they can do to earn extra money).

8. If you're self-employed or have a family business, hiring kids allows you to deduct their pay, which is also income tax-free to them up to $4,250.

9. Encourage kids to launch their own enterprise, based on their unique interests and talents.

Chapter 2

Saving and Investing

for Tots to Teens

FINANCIAL SUCCESS IS NOT JUST THE RESULT OF HOW much money a person earns, but how well she manages what she has. Former personal financial counselor Joan Cramer, now vice president of marketing for Greenfield Savings Bank in Greenfield, Massachusetts, recalls some of her former high-income professional clients had serious trouble living within their means. "One client and her husband, who together earn a couple hundred thousand dollars a year, had to mortgage their house in order to pay down their $80,000 credit-card debt from regular catalog shopping sprees. Sadly, now they have a mortgage, their credit-card balances are beginning to grow again, and they still have no savings."

The first step to managing and investing money is setting some aside—a discipline that few adults have mastered.
Don't let your own shortcomings prevent you from teaching
your kids to do better. As you read this chapter, you may
even find insight and inspiration for improving your own
approach to saving and investing—no matter how good or
bad a job you think you're already doing.

First, consider what saving is to you, to your children,
and to society.

When my son, Ryan, began to lobby for a new NBA
basketball jersey he saw on sale for $28, marked down from
$35, he argued, "We'll *save* $7 if we buy this one now!" He
looked at me quizzically when I responded, "We'll save $28
if we don't buy it at all!"

I explained, "Sales are great, but only when you pay
less for something you already planned to buy. When you
buy something you don't need, even if it is on sale really
really cheap, you are not saving, you are spending." He may
not have been totally convinced, but then again, even the
experts have a backward, derivative way of thinking about
saving.

Economists define saving as whatever portion of our
income we leave unspent (technically, personal disposable
income minus personal consumption expenditures). No
wonder we grown-ups have such a lousy track record. As a
nation, we are currently squirreling away about 4 percent of
our disposable income (after paying taxes). The United
States ranks a pitiful 16th out of 24 Western countries
(those of the 29 Organization of Economic Cooperation and
Development member countries that track saving rates).

If we are to help teach our children (and maybe, in the
process, ourselves) to develop discipline with setting aside
money, we need a less passive way of thinking about it. In
fact, we need to reverse the way we approach saving.

Instead of kids plunking whatever unspent money they
have left over into a piggy bank, bank account, or investment

vehicle, parents should guide them to decide on an appropriate amount or percent of income (from allowance, chores, gifts, and jobs) they will save, and then determine how much they will have left over for spending. Some financial experts refer to this as "paying yourself first." It is a highly recommended habit to get into for adults as well as kids.

Savings Incentives

THERE ARE MANY WAYS to encourage children to delay gratification and pay themselves first. Consider the following strategies you think might work for your family:

Require Children to Save a Set Amount of Income

One grandfather went so far as to tell his daughter and her two children that their individual inheritances will be tied to whatever amount they've saved by age 50. His estate will match that amount. He laments that his 8-year-old grandson "just spent $18 of savings on, would you believe, a new video game." [Gasp!] "You'd think that would be a strong incentive to save, but it rings on deaf ears. They must not think I mean it. And they will be surprised."

Actually, he may be the one surprised. The main thing we accomplish when we force our kids to save is to reduce their spending money. If allowance is intended to teach kids how to make decisions and trade-offs, forcing them to save is often counterproductive.

The trick is to keep rules about saving from feeling imposed. Joyce Christenbury, a family resource management and equipment specialist at Clemson University in Clemson, South Carolina, says, "If you establish a policy early on with a child and follow through, children don't see saving as forced and it becomes a normal procedure."

Make saving fun, celebrate saving. "People I've interviewed have vivid visual memories of saving as a child," says licensed psychologist Kathleen Gurney, Ph.D., CEO of

Financial Psychology in Sonoma, California. "They can remember what their bank looked like and where they kept it. Yet ask them to describe their first dress or toy, and they will often forget what it was." She likes to give Lucite™ money sorters for gifts. "It's fun to pop the coins in and it automatically sorts coins in the exact amount to fit into coin wrappers. It's difficult to acquire the habit of saving as an adult. If people are able to save as part of their daily routine, it becomes reflexive."

"I have never insisted (or even much encouraged) my kids to save," admits Rhonda Weide, a single mother of three in Wilsonville, Oregon. "Whatever they earn or are given is theirs to do with as they please. I simply let them know up front what I'll provide. They have to figure for themselves what they need to save if there is something special they want to do with their money."

So far, it seems to have worked. "They have saved and bought all their own bikes, ski equipment, stereos, etc., beginning when they were about 10 years old." Her 20-year-old daughter, on scholarship in college, worked during the summer so she could buy a new car. Weide's 24-year-old stepson just finished college, having paid all tuition costs himself without loans. He owns an assortment of grown-up toys, and invests in mutual funds and savings bonds. A 22-year-old son launched his own business instead of going to college—he has traveled the world, invests in oriental rugs, and has saved $16,000 for the down payment on a house.

Set Goals

Grown-ups have different reasons to save. Planned, short-term savings are for specific wants or needs, such as vacations, home electronics, and furniture. All too often, we *dis-save*—that is, purchase things with money we have yet to earn, on credit (discussed in Chapter 3). Regular, long-term savings is for expected future needs such as a new car, home improvements, college, and retirement. It also should include a rainy-day fund for unexpected sudden needs such as medical emergencies, car or house repairs, or to cover living expenses in the event we are unable to work.

For children, saving will also have more meaning if they have a goal—something *they* value, such as baseball cards, costume jewelry, sports equipment, or an electronic pet.

Children have a limited concept of time. Saving for the future, therefore, has little meaning, especially to kids younger than 6 or 7. Forcing them to save for the sake of it, or even for distant things like college, may not instill them with an appreciation for saving. Prof. Lynn White, a family economics specialist at Texas A&M University's Extension, recommends encouraging young kids with very short-term goals—something they can get in a week if they save their pennies and nickels. They can save for candy, perhaps balloons, or a little note pad, for instance. Then move to bigger goals that might take two weeks to save up for; later, a month.

"Keep their goals and progress visible and in front of them," suggests White, author of *Consumer Critters*, a money-management syllabus for kids. When a child decides to save up for, say, a $6 Barbie doll outfit advertised in a toy store circular, you can have her cut out the picture and tape it to a clear glass jar, so she can see the money accumulate inside. Then create a chart for them to record their progress, with stacks of however many quarters or dollars they need to save, which they can color in or circle as they make "deposits" into their jar.

Check out the Web page of First Technology Bank in Beaverton, Oregon (www.1sttech.com/kidsclb/kidscalc. html), for a fun way to calculate how much kids would need to save each month to buy different items. The page lists several items and typical prices, such as movie and popcorn ($10), computer software ($40), home video game ($50), bike ($125), rollerblades ($150), or snowboard ($400), or kids can enter a specific amount for whatever else they might dream of buying. Then they click one of three time-frames for saving (6, 12, or 18 months) and hit "calculate," and the screen shows how much the child has to save each month (it assumes the money will earn 2.5 percent annual interest in a passbook savings account). For instance, you need to save $20.68 a month for six months to save up for the $125 new bike; or $32.89 a month for a year to buy that new snowboard.

"The important lesson for kids to learn about saving—something many parents have yet to learn—is that they are in control," says White. When kids can't afford something they want, "they often feel like it's someone's fault or lack of income. They don't realize they make choices: if they buy this, they'll have to wait longer to get something else."

Inevitably, every so often the child will be tempted to blow all of a week's allowance on something else. "The parent can say, 'It's your choice, but know that if you buy this, you'll wait longer to get what you're saving for,'" adds White. Even if they choose to satisfy their immediate urge, they will begin to develop a sense of control over their financial choices and restrictions.

Pay Matching Grants

Amy, mother of 10- and 12-year-olds, matches dollar for dollar what her kids put in their passbook savings account. Tia's 6-year-old son enjoys going to the bank each Saturday with his father. His parents leave it up to him how much of his $3 weekly allowance he'll put into the bank, knowing his father will match the amount. He usually puts in $2.

Cindy Swikard, who co-owns with her husband a landscape construction company and a travel agency in San Diego, opened a savings account, with an initial deposit of $500, for each of her six kids (ages 12 to 17) when each one turned 10. "Any money they put in the account from the time they were 10 until they turned 16 we would match. We told them if they saved their money, they would be able to buy a car when they turned 16. This money is theirs; they have access to it. But if they take money out of this account, they must replace it before we start matching it again." The 17-year-old bought a $100 pair of sunglasses right after he got his account and tapped into it over the years. Now he has $400 and can't afford a car. His 16-year-old sister has saved more than $3,000. "Except for the oldest, the system has worked very well," says Swikard.

"The matching proportion can be 2:1 or 1:1, or any ratio you choose," says family therapist Kenneth Kaye, Ph.D. "Set it according to children's ages and earning capacity, how important the goal is to them, and how much you're willing to contribute."

Like setting goals, paying matching grants is more likely to work when the time horizons are short, especially for younger children. The grandfather mentioned earlier, whose estate will match whatever his daughter and grandchildren have saved by the time they turn 50, has discovered that an 8-year-old is unlikely to fathom, let alone feel motivated by, matching grants far into the future.

Tempering Little Hoarders

There are, of course, some kids who are so intent on saving that they find it hard to let go of a cent. Lake Alfred, Florida–based certified financial planner Grady Cash calls it the "Scrooge Syndrome." In his book, *Spend Yourself Rich* (Financial Literacy Center, 1997), Cash explains that some people "get so obsessed with saving they won't buy even needed items . . . . In severe cases, the Scrooge Syndrome can cause some real concerns for family members and it is obviously not a healthy attitude toward money."

Donna and Sid Levine of New Haven, Connecticut, sired two scrooges, Ilana, 10, and Josh, 8, who save just about all of their $2.50 per week allowances. Not only do they resist shelling out money for themselves, but also for family members. "We're trying to make them more generous with their money," says Donna. A couple years ago they decided not to buy Josh and Ilana a present one of the eight nights of Hanukkah—they had to buy presents for each other that night instead. "At first they didn't like that, but it became fun. When we take them to the store and they find something really perfect, just little things, they become excited." One year Ilana bought her brother Spiderman underpants and Josh found peanut butter and jelly ChapStick for his sis.

If you notice scroogelike qualities in your child, it's important to understand why they are acting that way, suggests licensed psychologist Kathleen Gurney. "It could stem from a sense of abandonment or lack of control. Often hoarders are worriers, who are hypercritical of themselves and others. They may have been raised with a lot of fears, not necessarily about money. Money can become a safety net for them, a way to protect themselves. Some can't spend because they feel they can never find the perfect shirt, vacation, or investment. They need to learn that mistakes are okay. Little scrooges can also be taught to give of themselves as well as their money. There are other ways to give, besides money.

"Sit down and talk to them about how it feels for them to spend money. Ask them why they want to save. What are they saving for? How much do they think they need to save? You can help them negotiate their own behaviors. If their feelings are unexpressed, they wind up acting them out. Talking about your own way of spending money, about how you choose what to buy, can help them learn how to make decisions. They won't change overnight, but it's important to begin working with them at an early age."

Little hoarders are often very good at manipulating parents into buying things for them so they don't have to use their own money. It's much easier for them to spend someone else's money than their own. Don't do it, warns

Gurney, lest your children develop a sense of entitlement and false expectations about the world. They will likely have difficulty later in life, when they will need to learn how to make decisions and trade-offs with family members, especially their future spouse.

Show How Money Saved Can Grow

Between their sixth and eighth year, you can begin to explain to your children that three things make money grow when it is deposited in a savings or investment account:

- Interest rate (how much the bank or investment will pay for the use of deposited money)
- Time (how long you leave it deposited)
- Compounding (when you keep your savings and interest in your account, you earn interest not just on the dollars you deposit, but also on the interest itself)

There are many nifty formulas, tables, and charts that illustrate what happens by depositing their cash instead of spending it.

Compound interest vs. simple interest

For instance, if you or your child deposit $1,000 into a bank account that pays 4 percent compound interest

---

TABLE 2.1

The Making of a Millionaire

Age	5	10	15	25	30	40
Monthly Investment*	$21.05	$34.70	$57.25	$156.82	$261.21	$747.45

* Assumes a hypothetical 10 percent annual rate of return before taxes, compounded monthly, with dividends reinvested. Share price and total return of an investment will fluctuate. This example is not intended to be representative of any SteinRoe fund.

Source: Liberty Securities Corporation

TABLE 2.2

The Power of Doubling a Penny a Day

Day	Amount	Day	Amount
1	$0.01	16	$327.68
2	$0.02	17	$655.36
3	$0.04	18	$1,310.72
4	$0.08	19	$2,621.44
5	$0.16	20	$5,242.88
6	$0.32	21	$10,485.76
7	$0.64	22	$20,971.52
8	$1.28	23	$41,943.04
9	$2.56	24	$83,886.08
10	$5.12	25	$167,772.16
11	$10.24	26	$335,544.32
12	$20.48	27	$671,088.64
13	$40.96	28	$1,342,177.28
14	$81.92	29	$2,684,354.56
15	$163.84	30	$5,368,709.12

Source: Liberty Financial Companies, *Young Investor Parent's Guide*

annually, at the end of year one you will have a total of $1,000 + 40 = $1,040. That $40 the bank pays is called simple interest. If, instead, this account compounds interest monthly, at the end of the year the money would have grown to $1,072.14.

"If you deposit $2,000 at the birth of a child into an account that earns 10 percent a year, and just let that money sit, then if one ignores tax considerations, that child would be able to retire at age 65 as a millionaire!" says Jerry Mason, associate professor at Texas Tech University's Family Financial Planning Center for Financial Responsibility.

For hopeful millionaires who are way past birth, *Table 2.1* on the previous page shows how much you need to invest every month to have $1 million by age 65.

Here's a fun and simple way to teach children about

compounding. Ask if he or she would rather have $20 today or a penny today that doubles in value every day for a month. As *Table 2.2, left*, demonstrates, you should pray your kids ask to pocket the $20—otherwise, you'll be out a cool $5.4 million at the end of the month!

You can even try illustrating this more tangibly by getting a roll of pennies from the bank and asking your kids, if you put a penny in the first square of a checkerboard and double the number of pennies in the next one and kept doing that, how many of the board's 64 squares would it take to finish the roll of pennies? (You'd run out before the seventh square!)

Rule of 72

Divide the interest rate into 72. The answer tells you how many years it will take your savings to double when you receive compound interest. For instance, $100 deposited in an 8 percent savings bond will take nine years ($72 \div 8 = 9$) to grow to $200.

Young children instinctively understand the advantage of stuffing their coins and bills under the mattress, or into a piggy bank or jar—they can have access to their

---

TABLE 2.3:

The Rule of 72

Interest Rate (Percent)	Years to Double Your Money
5	14.4
6	12.0
7	10.3
8	9.0
9	8.0
10	7.2

money any time they want it. That's called liquidity. For little big spenders, though, instant liquidity will likely melt away most of their savings. Instead, putting money in a bank or investment account helps their money grow. But how can you help your kids decide how to invest the money they save?

Investing

ONCE YOUR KIDS BEGIN saving, it's time to explain to them the many choices they have, from bank accounts to government savings bonds, to shares of individual companies or shares of a mutual fund that owns stocks of many companies. You don't already have to be a financial wiz to orient your kids. This chapter provides enough information and references to get you and your children off and running.

The important thing is to get started. Children have a fabulous edge when it comes to investing: a long time frame in which to let their money grow. By helping them capitalize on this advantage, you will set them up to have not only maximum future dollars, but also the knowledge and confidence to maneuver in the world when they eventually go out on their own. The most effective way to take advantage of kids' long time horizon is for them to practice "dollar cost averaging," in which investors deposit a set amount (as little as $50) a month into their investment vehicle, whether the market is up or down. You can explain to them that when the market is up, your monthly investment will buy fewer shares; when it is down you can buy more. This technique will produce higher returns than trying to catch every peak and valley.

As soon as your child shows any interest in saving or making money, there are fun ways to start getting her used to and comfortable with making financial decisions. Games such as Pit, for ages 8 and up (Parker Brothers, $9.95), can get everyone learning together. The card game teaches kids about what a commodity and exchange are, how to corner a market, and the difference between a bull and a bear. (The game is more fun with five or more players to bid against.) The best way to grab kids' interest in investing is to tell them about your own investments. Attorney, financial planner, stockbroker, and radio talk-show host Adriane Berg exposed her son, Arthur Berg Bochner, to financial dinner-table talk from the start. Arthur began investing at age 10. By the time he was 14, the value of his portfolio reached $100,000. The two coauthored the book *Totally Awesome Money Book for Kids and Their Parents* (Newmarket Press, 1993).

"When my wife and I talk investments and my sons come in the room, we don't hush our conversation. I talk about everything I do," says George Runkle, an engineer and self-taught investor, who writes in the on-line investment site, The Motley Fool (www.fool.com/). "It tends to spur some interest by my sons, and they ask questions about what we discuss. We also try to keep everything at a level they understand."

There are many places to invest; each option has benefits and drawbacks: in general, the greater the potential return, the more risk and/or less accessibility to the money (liquidity) you must accept. Even young kids can usually understand that the higher the risk and the longer they are willing to keep their money tied up in the investment, the more interest they are likely to earn.

The first decision investors must make concerns asset allocation—the portion of money placed in the stock (equity) market, corporate or government bonds, and cash (bank or money market accounts). Most experts recommend holding some of each. Stocks, which can have sudden gyrations in price, may have high long-term returns, but they can be risky in the short run. Investors should only keep the portion of their funds in stocks that they are unlikely to need to access quickly. The rest can be in less risky types of securities.

Banks and Other Savings Institutions

It's easy to take even very young children on a trip to the branch where you do your banking and explain to them what kinds of transactions you are making (deposits, withdrawals, transfers) and why. As they get a little older, you can have them fill in deposit or withdrawal slips, especially once they open their first savings account.

Until children reach the age of majority in their state, the only way they can have a bank, brokerage, or other investment account in their name is through a custodial account, which an adult opens in his or her name for a child (please see Chapter 3, "Keeping Track," and Chapter 5, "In Whose Name Should You Save?" for more details).

A fun and informative bank for kids is the Young Americans Bank (303-321-2265), based in Denver. It's not as convenient to open the account and make deposits as taking a stack of bills or coins to the neighborhood branch (unless you live in Denver). But Young Americans Bank specializes in serving the needs of children under the age of 18. Customers receive easy-to-understand booklets with many activities and fun facts about money. Its 17,000 accounts from youth around the country have more than $8.5 million in deposits—and growing—with an average balance of $500. This kid-friendly bank, which also offers certificates of deposit, checking accounts, ATM cards, travelers' checks, credit cards, and even personal loans, provides a hands-on learning experience.

Here are the basic types of bank accounts and some facts you can explain to your kids about them:

■ *Savings accounts* (low rate, low risk, high liquidity) keep money we save safe, as they are federally insured up to $100,000 (per customer, not per account). Savings accounts also pay interest—a little extra money for letting the bank use the money until we want it back. When we make a deposit, the bank pools our money with money from other savers, and uses it to make loans to people (to buy a car or house) and businesses (to buy supplies for making their products). When we want some or all of our money back, we can get it anytime the bank is open. We won't get back the exact same bills and coins we deposited, but we can get the exact same amount, plus whatever interest we have earned.

There are many kinds of savings accounts. One of the most common is a passbook savings account, which gives owners a record book they bring each time they put in or take out money so the bank can keep track of each transaction and how much is in the account. With a statement savings account, instead of a passbook the bank will mail you each month or every three months a list of your transactions and how much is left.

■ *Checking accounts* (low or no rate, low risk, instant liquidity) are actually a vehicle for spending, not saving. They allow people to write checks up to the amount they have deposited into it. It is a convenient way to access your money at little or no cost on most accounts, but unless you keep a lot of money in the account, you probably won't earn interest.

Most bank accounts today come with cards for automatic teller machines, or ATMs, which allow you to withdraw from or deposit money into your account at many locations in your town, and even in other states or countries, at any hour of the day or night. When you use yours in the presence of your kids, make sure to remind them that you can only take out money that you have already put in, and that transactions are usually limited to $300 a day. With kids 10 and older, you can also point out how the "available balance" may include more cash in the account. Some banks add in an overdraft protection amount that the bank account owner can borrow (at a high interest rate).

■ *Certificate of deposits* (medium rate, low risk, limited liquidity), or CDs, also called time deposits, pay a guaranteed amount of interest on money we deposit, which we

TABLE 2.4

Features of Bank Accounts

Type of account	Will I earn interest?	May I write checks?	Any withdrawal limitations?	Are fees likely?
Regular checking	No	Yes	No	Yes
Interest checking (NOW)	Yes	Yes	No	Yes
Money market deposit account (MMDA)	Yes, usually higher than NOW or savings	Yes, 3 per month	Yes, 6 per month	Yes
Savings	Yes	No	Same as MMDA	Yes
Certificate of deposit (CD)	Yes, usually higher than MMDA	No	Yes, usually no withdrawals until maturity	Yes, if you withdraw principal before maturity

Source: "Making Sense of Savings," by the Board of Governors of the Federal Reserve System

must let the bank keep for a specific amount of time (days, weeks, months, or even several years). The longer we are willing to let the bank keep the money, the higher the interest the bank pays us. If we need the money we deposited (called the principal) before the time period is up (called maturity), we usually have to pay the bank a penalty. Some CDs allow you to withdraw interest you have earned so far without paying a penalty, but not the principal.

■ *Money market deposit accounts* (a little higher rate than savings account, low risk, high liquidity) are like a combination of a savings and checking account. They pay higher interest than regular savings and checking accounts and let you write checks, but you usually have to keep a lot of money in the account, called a minimum balance.

Table 2.4, left, compares the features of different types of bank accounts.

Stock Market

The stock market presents an opportunity to tie investing to your kids' interests. George Runkle's younger son, Jay, 10, loves trains. "P/E ratios [a stock's per share price divided by the company's per share earnings] fail to interest him. Instead of force-feeding him numbers, we bought him some stock in Norfolk Southern. When the annual reports come, we hand them to Jay, and he looks at the pictures. We stress to him that he owns part of a railroad, which he is really proud of." Runkle and his wife keep Jay informed about how the stock is performing. "As he grows older, he'll be able to comprehend investing in greater depth. We have plenty of time, we don't need to force him to be a child investment prodigy."

Indeed, his 14-year-old "loves to talk to me about P/E ratios, expected earnings growth, and so on. He also has stock that he chose in Boeing and Raytheon"—airplanes are his passion. "Watching his investments rise in value gives him an incentive to want to invest. He also has followed those companies carefully, and learned about business and the stock market."

Runkle adds, "I shared with my sons my early mistakes. My older son thought it was hilarious when I lost all of my $500 investment in Morrison Knudsen, a construction engineering company I bought two and a half years ago when it was having financial problems. I'm an engineer, so I thought it would be a good investment for me. But I didn't know anything about finances. Then I read the company's 10K report, which described the company's trouble winning projects and getting bonding. Had I read it before, I never would have bought the stock. About six months later, the value of my investment fell to half and I sold my shares.

"As if I hadn't had enough punishment, I then read that Morrison Knudson brought in someone from Chrysler as CEO. The stock price jumped a little, so I bought $200 worth, figuring that's what it would cost me to gamble in Atlantic City. Sure enough, I lost it all.

"My son brings this up every chance he gets. Hopefully, he learned not to make the same mistake of investing before reading about a company's financial health."

For parents who are not confident of their own knowledge, teaching kids about the stock market can feel daunting. One way to start learning with your children is to send away for and read *Ump's Fwat: An Annual Report for Young People* ($5, published by sports equipment and fire-safety equipment company Figgie International and the Academy for Economic Education, Richmond, Virginia, 804-643-0071). *Ump's Fwat* is the story of an enterprising prehistoric guy named Ump who figures out there is a demand for baseball-batlike clubs. It describes how he starts producing and selling them, later earning enough to hire employees, and eventually selling shares of the company to his neighbors, who earn a percent of Ump's profits.

In *The Stock Market Explained for Young Investors*, by Clayton P. Fisher (Business Classics, 1993), the 17-year-old author imparts technical aspects of investing in simple language geared for teens serious about investing.

Direct investing

Here are four tips for young investors from Joan Morrissey, who teaches money management and investing to her seventh-grade students in Arlington, Massachusetts. Much of what she says would work for interested fifth and even fourth graders:

1. Encourage your kids to pick the stock of a company they can relate to, such as Hasbro, Campbell Soup, or

Eastman Kodak. She recommends you help them find one with a share price low enough for them to afford one or two shares, and that offers a dividend reinvestment plan (see the section on DRIPs). Explain that when you buy a stock, you own a piece of the company and get part of the profit.

2. Help your kids write to that company for information, including an annual report. I would add that when it comes, browse through it together. I know, I know, many parents have a hard time following the content of an annual report. You don't need to launch into a discussion about balance sheets and cash flow. But you can at least check in the front how the company performed in the most recent year, compared with the year before. Did sales and profit go up or down? Has the stock price increased as much as market indicators such as the Dow Jones Industrial Average? Most annual reports have glossy color photos of the company's products and facilities that can help your child get a sense of the company. Answer questions they may have that you happen to know, and write down the questions you cannot answer. Then go to the reference room of your library together or visit Liberty Financial's Web site (www.younginvestor.com), where you and your child can look up the things you don't know in language that you both are likely to understand.

3. Show your child how to look up the price of his or her stock in the newspaper. You can explain that many factors affect the daily price fluctuations, such as inflation, interest rates, demand for that company's products and services, the price of supplies that the company must buy to make its product or deliver its service, competition, changing consumer tastes, the health of the economy, and the whims of investors. Tell them that although stock prices will go up and down, over time the price will rise if the company can sell more of what it makes. In case you're a bit rusty on reading stock tables, *Tables 2.5* and *2.6*, on the following page, will refresh your memory.

TABLE 2.5

Stock Market Table Excerpt

52-Week High	52-Week Low	Stock	Div	Yield percent
85⅛	59⅞	Disney	.53	0.7
52⅞	32½	Reebok	.30	0.6
38⅞	25½	RJRNab	2.05	6.3
45¼	33⅜	**SaraLee**	**.84**	**1.7**

TABLE 2.6:

How to Read the Stock Tables

52-Week High (and Low): The highest (and lowest) the stock reached in the previous 52 weeks demonstrates the stock's volatility—an indicator of upside profit potential and downside risk. Percent matters more than dollars here. For instance, Disney's 25¼-point spread represents a 42 percent price fluctuation, while Reebok's 20⅜-point spread is a wider 63 percent fluctuation, which means its stock price is more volatile than Disney's.

Stock: The tables usually list companies alphabetically, by abbreviation. If you can't figure out the company you want to look up by the abbreviated names on the table, you can call the business editor of your local newspaper or a broker, or check one of many Web sites, such as FinanceCenter (www.networth.galt.com), which allows you to look up company stock prices by company name or its abbreviated name (also called its ticker symbol).

Div: Many companies pay shareholders a dividend, a portion of the company's profit for each share they own. In this case, Disney has been paying shareholders an annual 53 cents per share. Dividends are often paid quarterly. When a company increases its dividend, it is a sign that management is optimistic about its future. When the dividend column for a

P/E	Sales 100s	High	Low	Last	Chg
29	62892	80¼	76¾	79¹⁵/₁₆	+2¹³/₁₆
23	15711	49⁷/₁₆	46⅞	49¼	+2¹¹/₁₆
12	71050	33¹³/₁₆	32⁶/₁₆	32¹¹/₁₆	-1⅜
25	**219423**	**50½**	**45⅛**	**49¹⁵/₁₆**	**+7⅜**

company is blank, that means the company does not pay cash dividends.

Yld percent: The percent yield tells you how much dividend you get for what you would pay for a share of the stock today. Disney's 53-cent dividend represents a yield of seven-tenths of a percent of its stock price—way below interest rates you could earn on many other investments.

P/E: The price-earnings ratio expresses the relationship between the current price of one share of stock and the company's annual earnings per share. The price of RJR Nabisco's stock is 12 times its earnings per share, while Disney's price is 29 times its earnings. The higher the P/E, the more you are paying for a given dollar of earnings.

Sales 100s: This figure, times 100, is the number of shares traded the previous day, also known as volume. For instance, more than 219 million shares of Sara Lee were bought and/or sold. The listing for Sara Lee is underlined to indicate it experienced an unusual volume of trading.

Hi, Low, and Last: These columns show the highest, lowest, and closing price of the stock for the previous day.

Chg: This tells you how much the closing price is up or down over the previous day's closing price. *Table 2.5* shows that RJR Nabisco was down 1⅜ points, while Sara Lee was up 7⅜ points (it's in bold to highlight that it had a price change of 5 percent or more).

4. Teach your child how to graph a stock's progress. You can do this for price changes over any interval, but once a week is manageable in terms of time and keeping up their interest. Track the price on graph paper or on the computer. Many on-line services let you create a portfolio: you list the stocks and the number of shares you own and it updates the price of each and total portfolio value. FinanceCenter's Web page (www.networth.galt.com) charts the year-to-date price of any stock, or its 10-year ups and downs, and will plot its price against stock market indexes such as the Dow Jones Industrial Average and Standard & Poor's 500 Stock Index.

DRIPs

Buying "odd lots," or small amounts of shares, can be extremely expensive. Brokerage fees could even exceed the cost of a share or two of stock. An easy and affordable way to get started is through a dividend reinvestment plan (DRIP), also called direct investment plans. About 1,100 U.S. corporations sell shares directly through DRIPs, with little if any transaction fee. Most programs let you start with as little as one share. *The Moneypaper Guide to Dividend Reinvestment Plans*, published by Temper the Times Communications and the Moneypaper ($27, 800-388-9993), provides information on more than 1,100 DRIPs, including how to enroll, register, build a portfolio, minimum and maximum investments accepted, phone numbers, and recent company price and performance. Your kids may be especially interested in the DRIP companies listed in *Table 2.7, right,* which may have more name recognition and meaning to children.

Most DRIP stocks require you to purchase the first share through a broker, and you will have to pay a commission on that share. Make sure that you tell the broker to issue that share under your kid's name and Social Security number. If you don't, most brokers hold your shares in a "street" account under their firm's name. You can't enroll in a DRIP unless the stock is in the shareholder's name.

TABLE 2.7:

DRIPs with Kiddie Appeal

The following are 11 high-growth stocks that are kid-friendly, have low or no fees, offer easy access, and are a good investment.

Campbell Soup (201-324-0498)

Coca-Cola (888-265-3747)

Delta Airlines (201-324-1225)

Eastman Kodak (800-253-6057)

Hasbro (800-733-5001)

H. J. Heinz (800-253-3399)

Johnson & Johnson (800-328-9033)

Kellogg (800-323-6138)

K-Mart (800-336-6981)

Sara Lee (800-554-3406)

Wendy's International (800-278-4353)

Source: The Moneypaper Guide to Dividend Reinvestment Plans (Temper the Times Communications, Inc.)

Good resources on DRIPs include two books by Charles B. Carlson: *Buying Stocks Without a Broker* (McGraw-Hill, 1996, $17.95), and *No-Load Stocks: How to Buy Your First Share and Every Share Directly from the Company—With No Brokers Fee* (McGraw-Hill, 1997, $16.95).

Other pamphlets worth ordering for novice investors:

■ *Investor's Bill of Rights,* by the National Futures Association (Free, 800-621-3570 or 800-572-9400 in Illinois), addresses the rights and responsibilities of buyers and sellers of investments, including honesty in advertising, full and accurate information, disclosure of risks, and explanation of obligations and costs.

■ *Invest Wisely, Advice from Your Securities Industry*

Regulators, by the U.S. Securities and Exchange Commission (Cost: $0.50, 202-942-7040), explains how to choose a brokerage firm and broker, how to make investment decisions, track an investment, and deal with a problem concerning your account or your broker.

Simulated investing

If you'd like to teach your kids about the stock market but are not ready or able to invest, there are many ways to simulate investing. If you have access to the Internet, Chicago brokerage firm Stein Roe & Farnham has some stock market games at its Web site (www.young investor.com).

Not all information and activities on the Internet, even from an established institution, are beneficial. The Securities Industry Foundation for Economic Education in New York City (212-608-1500) has its Stock Market Game on the Internet (www.smg2000.org), intended for groups of students (grades 4 to 12) in a class to play, each with a hypothetical $100,000 to invest for 10 weeks. Although kids who play this game undoubtedly learn a lot about investing, some of the lessons may be counterproductive, suggests Bill Wood, professor of economics at James Madison University in Harrisonburg, Virginia. "Students have to engage in highly speculative strategies if they're going to have a chance of winning," he notes. "For example, diversification is an obvious principle for someone investing in real life. That's the kiss of death for a Stock Market Game team."

In addition, the short-term nature of the game is counter to the concept of long-term investing. Wood also points out that investing is quite different when you risk your own real money. Although the game book includes information about socially responsible investing, the game does not emphasize the pros and cons of investing in environmentally friendly firms or avoiding liquor producers. He says the game rewards high portfolio value and does not reward socially responsible investments. You can win by buying tobacco companies or arms dealers. The Stock Market Game also ignores one of the safest, least expensive, and easiest ways for individuals to invest—mutual funds (see section on mutual funds). Kids also need to know that in reality, stock appreciation is paper profit until investors sell the stock (and pay tax on their gains). With all this in mind, teachers and parents of kids who play the game can emphasize how actual investing differs from this simulation.

Don't despair if you don't have Internet access. Just give your kids a hypothetical amount of money to start with, say $1,000, and help them select stocks that sound interesting. You and your young capitalists can look up important measures of how financially healthy that company is with a trip to the library. *Value Line, Standard & Poor's, Moody's Investment Guide,* and *Hoover's* are some of the many books that track the performance of public companies. Then tell your kids to pick the companies they have the most confidence in and to decide how many shares of each company to buy based on current prices listed in the newspaper, without exceeding their budget of $1,000. You can have fun every weekend tracking the price of each stock and the total value of their shadow portfolio.

Selena Maranjian, a feature writer, suggests in her column in The Motley Fool on-line site, that parents "scan newspapers and magazines for stories about the companies you're interested in. Is McDonald's promoting 55-cent burgers? Will this help the company by bringing in more sales, or will it hurt, by decreasing the total profit? And how did the stock market react when it heard of this announcement? Did the stock go up or down?"

Maranjian also recommends taking advantage of subjects of all sorts that kids can learn from investing:

■ Math: when stock prices in a real or simulated portfolio go up or down, help kids calculate how much money they made, what percent return they earned (previous price minus current price, divided by previous price).

■ History: examine how companies they're interested in got where they are now.

■ Science: can help explain what today's high-tech or health-care companies are doing.

■ English: they can read research about stocks and industries, and write why they are interested in a particular stock and why the company seems promising.

There are many measures of how well a stock is performing, including earnings per share, return on investment, and yield (see glossary of investment terms in *Table 2.8* on pages 70–71). Companies provide these figures in the form of the annual report, quarterly earnings reports, and other documents the government requires publicly owned companies to distribute to stockholders.

Of course, not all children will develop a passion for the stock market, and that's okay. They can still learn something about the world of finance and how money grows, and benefit from the growth of those investments. Donna and Sid Levine, the New Haven, Connecticut, couple, invested $5,000 for their oldest daughter, Sarah, 19, when she was 7. They picked 20 stocks that catered to kids, including Toys 'R' Us, Hershey, Disney, Wendy's, Kellogg, Heinz, Pillsbury (now owned by Gillette), Campbell Soup, and Coca Cola. "We bought 10 shares of each company," recalls Sid. "Their annual reports had pictures, and once in a while they sent coupons for their products. Disney had a nice picture of animated Disney characters on the stock certificate. But Sarah didn't show much interest in whether the price was going up or down." In 10 years, the portfolio, which they did not actively trade, grew to about $30,000. They have also invested money for their younger children, Ilana, 10 and Josh, 8. "They don't have the depth of portfolio that Sarah had, but they are much more interested in money and investing."

Investment clubs

Many families and classrooms pool their money and invest together in securities the club researches and jointly decides to purchase. Many clubs are comprised almost entirely of minors, although at least one adult member is needed to place brokerage orders and handle the tax forms. The National Association of Investors Corp. (NAIC) in Madison Heights, Michigan (248-583-6242), is an umbrella group for some 37,000 investment clubs (there are tens of thousands of other clubs not affiliated with NAIC). The NAIC provides its 735,000 club members (about 2,000 of whom are kids) with various manuals including a kids' manual called *Investing for Life* ($30 for members, $40 for nonmembers), computer software, videos, and other materials to help them make educated choices. Annual fees include $35 for the club plus $14 for each person. Look for a new youth investor program NAIC plans to launch by early 1999, which will include regional seminars, educational materials, and tools.

NAIC encourages its members to invest for the long term, diversify, reinvest dividends, and buy mostly blue-chip stocks such as Disney, Merck, Motorola, and Wal-Mart. Members, who each invest an average of $43 per month, have a pretty good track record—better, in fact, than many professional money managers. In 1997, 43 percent of all NAIC investment clubs that responded to NAIC's annual survey outperformed the S&P 500. Only 10.67 percent of mutual funds did so that year, according to CDA Investment Technologies.

The following sources can help you find an existing club (or guide you on starting one for your family and/or friends):

■ *The Beardstown Ladies' Common-Sense Investment Guide,* by The Beardstown Ladies' Investment Club with Leslie Whitaker (Hyperion, 1995, $19.95).

■ *Main Street Beats Wall Street: How the Top Investment Clubs are Outperforming the Investment Pros,* by Richard J. Maturi (Probus Publishing, 1994, $22.95).

■ *The Investment Club Book,* by John F. Waski (Warner Books, 1995, $12.99).

■ *The Money Club: How We Taught Ourselves the Secret to a Secure Financial Future, and How You Can, Too,* by Marilyn Crockett, Diane Felenstein, and Dale Burg (Simon & Schuster, 1997, $24.00).

■ *Starting and Running a Profitable Investment Club,* by Thomas E. O'Hara and Kenneth S. Janke Sr. (Times Business, 1998, $15.00).

Also check out this Web site (www.investorama.com), which lists some 50 on-line investment clubs, provides links to a directory of more than 7,500 investment sites in 80 categories, and has a directory of more than 4,500 public companies with Web sites.

The downside of most investment clubs is that members have to attend regular meetings (although an increasing number of clubs are cyberclubs that include members from around the country), develop a consensus about where to invest, take care of bookkeeping, track performance of stocks, research new picks, and prepare reports for members. To avoid fraud or even honest mistakes like the embarrassing overstatement of the Beardstown Ladies' investment performance discovered in early 1998, it's important that all members, not just the treasurer of the club, keep an eye on the club's financial statements. If you like the idea of pooled, diversified investments but are intimidated by the responsibilities of an investment club, consider mutual funds.

Mutual funds

As you've probably heard, a mutual fund is a simple and inexpensive way to invest in a diverse group of stocks, bonds, or other securities. Many adults as well as kids may not understand that mutual fund shareholders do not own the stocks and other securities in the fund, nor do they own any part of the mutual fund company. When you buy shares of a mutual fund, you are pooling your money with investments of thousands of other mutual fund shareholders. Mutual funds are attractive to kids for the same reason they are attractive to adult investors—unless you can commit to buying huge sums in a portfolio of individual stocks, you cannot achieve the same diversity and would have to pay higher commissions. There are more mutual funds than there are companies listed on the New York Stock Exchange, so be as cautious picking one as you would be selecting a stock. Many funds specialize in specific industries or types of investment, such as tax-deferred or tax-free securities, precious metals, and international stocks. Index funds buy only the stocks of a particular index, like the Dow Jones Industrial Average or the S&P 500, hoping to match the performance of these indexes. Megafunds (funds of funds) only buy shares in other mutual funds. There are even two funds that specialize in young investors:

■ Stein Roe Young Investor Fund (800-338-2550) invests primarily in the stocks of companies kids are familiar with (Nike, Microsoft, etc.) and is devoted to educating (and capturing) young investors. For instance, the prospectus (a legal document that describes a fund's or stock's investment objectives, policies, restrictions, officers, directors, and expenses) is written at about the seventh-grade level. Shareholders also receive a quarterly newsletter, the *Dollar Digest*, which includes profiles of companies and their chief executives, such as Microsoft's Bill Gates, as well as contests, surveys, and investment tips.

The fund requires a $100 minimum investment for those who set up an automatic investment plan of at least $50 a month; or a $1,000 minimum without the automatic investment plan on custodial accounts for minors. All other accounts require a $2,500 minimum. People who invested in the fund when it started in 1994 saw their money double by

1997. The fund's Web page (www.steinroe.com) includes investment games and financial information that you can look up in reference areas.

■ USAA's First Start Growth (800-531-0553) has a lower $250 minimum investment for custodial accounts,

---

TABLE 2.8

Glossary of Investment Terms

Refer to the following list of basic terms as you introduce your kids to the world of investing.

Appreciation—an increase in the value of a commodity or a security.

Blue chips—elite companies that are considered solid stock investments, named after the most valuable poker chips.

Bond—a security in which the investor essentially lends a municipality or a company money (principal) for a set amount of time (maturity) during which the issuer pays the investor a percent of the principal (interest). When bonds are traded on the secondary market (as opposed to purchased "new" from the issuing company), the yield (described below) will increase when the price drops (because when you pay less than the initial, or par, price you still get the same percent interest, based on the par price).

Compounding—when investors keep interest payments in an account, allowing that interest to earn future interest along with the money they have invested in that account.

Depreciation—a decrease in value.

Dividend—please see description under how to read the stock tables in *Table 2.6*.

Earnings per share—a company's net earnings (or profit) divided by the total number of shares of stock outstanding.

Interest—a percentage of invested or loaned dollars that a bank or borrower pays for the use of those dollars.

Liquidity—the degree to which money we have deposited in and no minimum for those who make automatic monthly investments as low as $20. First Start also provides educational literature, as well as an account document folder that helps kids (and parents) get into the habit of properly filing deposit slips, statements, and related documents.

an account is available when we want it back.

Load—fees mutual fund companies charge when you buy shares of the fund.

Maturity—the date an investment, security, or loan is set to be repaid.

Mutual fund—a portfolio of investment securities (stocks and/or corporate or government bills and bonds) that is owned by a group of investors who pool their money together to benefit from increased diversification.

Portfolio—the stocks, bonds, and other securities owned by an investor.

Price-earnings ratio (P/E)—the current listed price of a share of stock divided by that company's current earnings per share. The result shows how much "the market" (buyers and sellers of stocks) has factored into the market price the company's future expected growth. Generally, the higher the P/E, the less potential for significant further appreciation (unless that company or industry becomes the object of a fad).

Principal—the initial amount of a loan or deposit in a bank account.

Return—what you earn in interest or dividends and appreciation, divided by the amount of your initial investment, expressed as a percentage.

Stock—a unit of ownership of a company, which entitles the owner to a share of the company's earnings and assets.

Yield—in stocks, how much dividend you get for what you would pay for each share today; in bonds, the effective interest rate on a bond based on its current price (as the market price goes up, the yield drops because the actual interest is a fixed percent of the original issue price of the bond).

People saving for college, if they have enough time left, like to buy funds that emphasize long-term appreciation, such as high-growth stock funds. These can be a bit riskier in the short term, but have a good chance of achieving high returns. People at or near retirement prefer funds comprised of stocks with high dividends that provide current income. Instead of reinvesting those dividends to take advantage of future compounding, these investors need the cash now, to pay for immediate living expenses.

Most experts recommend sticking to no-load mutual funds, which do not charge for purchasing or selling their shares (both Young Investor Fund and First Start Growth Fund are no-load). Load funds can charge commissions as high as 8.5 percent. Both load and no-load funds, though, do charge an annual management fee, usually 0.05 to 1 percent of the value of your mutual fund shares. Some funds have much higher fees, so be sure to check the prospectus or ask the fund's telephone representative to quote you the total fee. Remember, less than 11 percent of mutual funds outperformed the S&P 500 Index—so choose your funds carefully.

Internet buffs can find lots of information on-line. NETworth's site (www.networth.galt.com) has a directory of mutual funds and a list of the past year's 25 best-performing funds in about 45 categories. Other investment sites for kids and adults are listed in the appendix.

Jennifer Gerald, a stay-at-home mom from Goose Creek, South Carolina, bought funds for her children, ages 3$^{1}/_{2}$, 7, 10, and 12. She says her husband "did the researching of the mutual funds and tried explaining it to the kids, which was too hard. Then he showed them some of our statements, and the older children liked the idea of turning money into more money, and not doing anything. We receive quarterly reports from the company—each child's is addressed to them. They like getting the mail and seeing how their money has grown. Our oldest son came back from a long visit with family and had earned some money mowing lawns. We had no idea he had earned money while on vacation; he could have easily not told us. He gave us half to put into his fund." Even the youngest is catching on. "My 3-year-old son just found some coins on the floor and said to me in his most serious toddler voice, 'Mommy, will you put these in my mootool fund?'"

The New Commonsense Guide to Mutual Funds by Mary Rowland (Bloomberg Press, 1998) provides an in-depth tour and tips for smart investing. Invest Wisely: An Introduction to Mutual Funds, published by the U.S. Securities and Exchange Commission (202-942-7040), is a quick-and-dirty description of how mutual funds work that you can use to beef up on personal finance so you can clue in your kids, much as you might cram on science and math to help your kids with homework.

WHEN KIDS LEAVE HOME with a financial cushion of their own making, they can be proud of their accomplishment. They can also be confident in their ability to set and reach goals, which will pay them more dividends than any stock you could give them.

Focus first and foremost on getting your kids in the habit of saving. They don't need to save an uncomfortable amount; better they squirrel away a little each time they receive money than big chunks haphazardly. Once they have demonstrated the ability to resist squandering, you can test their interest in investing. Let the degree and direction of their interest guide you.

TABLE 2.9
Saving and Investing Tips to Remember

1. Teach kids to "pay themselves first"—to decide on an appropriate amount or percent of income (from allowance, chores, gifts, and jobs) they will save, and *then determine* how much they will have left over for spending—instead of the other way around.

2. Help young kids set modest short-term goals—things they can save up for in a week. Then gradually encourage them to set progressively bigger goals that will take longer to save for.

3. Keep goals visible, with a picture of the desired object (especially for younger kids) and a chart (like a diagram of a thermometer) for tracking saving progress.

4. Expect and allow for occasional lapses in their saving plan.

5. For especially reluctant savers (or to reward good savers!), offer to pay a matching grant for however much they deposit in a savings account or mutual fund.

6. Make saving fun. Help them decorate their bank or give them a neat Lucite™ coin sorter. Celebrate their saving achievements.

7. Teach kids about investing by sharing with them your own investment decisions and results—including mistakes.

8. Guide them to make actual or simulated investments in companies related to their passions (sports equipment companies for sports fanatics, auto manufacturers for car enthusiasts).

Chapter 3

Teaching

Accountability for

Cash and Credit

ACCOUNTABILITY IS A VITAL PART OF FINANCIAL management and sanity. People who can't keep track of what they have undercut their own efforts to spend, save, and invest wisely. Being accountable is also a critical link in handling credit wisely, as you'll see later in this chapter.

George Washington's penchant for keeping painstakingly detailed logs of every penny spent on every farm and household implement helped him turn a modest Mount Vernon, which he inherited at age 20, into a thriving plantation.

There are all kinds of opportunities and methods to teach children accountability with money. What seems to matter more than which system you choose is that:

■ Your system "be clear, specific, with enforceable consequences," emphasizes Skokie, Illinois, psychologist Kenneth Kaye, Ph.D.

■ You are consistent with rules you impose about how much kids can save and spend, and what they can spend their money on. Even parents who give kids free rein to decide how much to save and spend should still hold them accountable for knowing how they've used their money.

■ You tie the specific freedoms and accountabilities to your strategic goals. For instance, if your purpose in giving an allowance is to enable your children to learn how to make trade-offs, you may not want to impose heavy-handed rules about how they spend it. But you can still require them to create a budget to track what they earn and spend, and help them set saving goals for things they want but can't afford.

Many kids are careless with their things, including money. Giving them money may become frustrating to you, and to them, if they lose it or have no idea how much they have. As soon as kids start handling even small sums of money, they therefore need two things: a safe, accessible place to keep it and a system for recording how much they have.

Where Does the Money Go?

MANY PARENTS SET UP a multibank system, with separate money containers for spending, long-term saving, short-term saving, and charitable giving. Just make sure that your kids can take bills and coins out of the containers they use—not one of those ceramic or plastic piggy banks with no plugged hole on the bottom. Especially for young children who handle mostly coins, a transparent jar allows them to see how much money they have and how it grows. As we mentioned in Chapter 2, a Lucite™ money sorter is especially fun and functional.

Josh Levine of New Haven, Connecticut, 8, made a

cardboard contraption with compartments for dollars, quarters, nickels, dimes, and pennies to stash his cash for several months. When his bank gets full he asks his parents to take him to the bank so he can deposit the cash in his passbook savings account.

Aleta Motzkus's kids, now ages 13, 14, 16, 19, and 20, have each had their own account for three years, which they monitor with a spreadsheet computer program. "If they keep their money in their room it seems to disappear. So I hold it. We have five columns: dates, transaction (where the money came from or where it went), credit, debit, and balance." Instead of handling cash, the kids enter the allowance they accrue on the computer. When they want to buy something, Motzkus gives them the cash and they post that transaction on the spreadsheet. "It has really helped them to see where their money comes from and where it goes," she says.

This system has some potential bugs. First, it depends on parents having ready cash whenever the kids need or want it. The problem is not just a matter of having enough cash, but also the exact amount. I have enough trouble remembering on Fridays to have enough singles to pay my 10-year-old his $4 allowance. Having the right amount on hand at any given moment to meet the kids' demands may prove frustrating for you and disappointing for them if you just don't have it (you could, I suppose, keep the allowance in an escrowlike box or jar in the house and plunk in their weekly allowance there). The second problem with holding onto your kids' cash is that it doesn't give them experience handling money. Kids who lose their coins or bills are more likely to develop more responsible ways of storing it if they suffer the consequences. In fact, if they are responsible enough to sit down to work a computer spreadsheet, they must be capable of physically dealing with cash.

I recommend a combination strategy: Let your kids handle cash, and ask them to keep track of it on paper or on a spreadsheet.

Keeping Track

WHETHER OR NOT YOUR KIDS get to keep their cash in their hot little hands, they should be held accountable for keeping track of its comings and goings. Computers offer a dependable way to do so (it's harder to lose your hard drive than a hand-written tally sheet). Software programs abound, including Intuit's Quicken 98 Basic ($39.95; 800-446-8848, www.quicken.com) and Microsoft Money 99 Basic ($34.95; 800-426-8080, www.microsoft.com). *Windows* magazine rates Quicken's program as slightly better. Most personal-finance software is geared for adults, but some account registers and spreadsheets are simple enough for techno-minded teens to use.

Many free Web sites can help you and your kids monitor investments. As we mentioned in Chapter 2, NETworth's site (www.networth.galt.com) can chart your stock's price over time and compare it to other stocks and indexes. It has a directory of mutual funds and a list of the past year's 25 best-performing funds. The site also lets you keep tabs on your investments in up to 10 personal portfolios and provides the latest news about your favorite companies.

Low-tech systems can be just as effective as computer programs. For preschoolers, you can create a chart or graph that depicts how much they have saved in their piggy bank. Once they are able to add and subtract, you can find an unused checkbook register and show kids (probably age 8 and over) how to record "deposits" into their piggy bank and "withdrawals" whenever they go on a spending spree. Encourage them (and show them how) to "reconcile" their balance each month with an actual counting of unspent coins and bills they have stashed away.

The more that you make this fun—in a light, no-pressure way—the more likely they will be to make a habit of dealing responsibly with money. If your child doesn't find it fun, pushing it will likely backfire. Consider another system, or drop it altogether for a while and try again in a year or so. Once kids save up more than $50 or $100, you may want to encourage them to open up a bank savings account. By law, minors cannot open bank or investment accounts by themselves until they have reached the age of majority, which varies from 18 to 21 depending on the state in which the child resides. Adults can, however, open a custodial account for children. The legal owner of the account is the child, but the custodial adult assumes fiduciary responsibility (which means the custodian is charged with managing the funds in the best interests of the child) until the child reaches the legal age of adulthood. (Please see Chapter 5, "In Whose Name Should You Save?" for more details.)

If you or some other adult opens a savings or checking account for your child, the statements will be mailed to the child. Once they are in third or fourth grade, you can teach them how to balance their account and reconcile their monthly or quarterly statements. Young Americans Bank (303-321-2265) in Denver publishes pamphlets for kids who open accounts on how to do that (especially *Now That You Have a Checking Account* and *Now That You Have a Savings Account*). If you're on-line, check out www.collegeboard.org (type "checkbook balancer" in the home page search engine), which shows how to balance a checkbook in five easy steps.

Not ready for the real thing? Just as we recommended simulated investing in Chapter 2, there are many ways to simulate banking. One way is for parents to hold their kids' allowance and act as banker, as Aleta Motzkus does. You can use unused checks and registers from old accounts to keep track of their money. When junior wants to cash a check to buy something, he writes a check and Mom or Dad shells out the money.

You don't have to be a Prodigy subscriber to access many fun and informative features on its Kids' Money page on the Web (pages.prodigy.com/kidsmoney/), which includes gobs of links to other kids and money sites.

Budgeting

MAKING — AND KEEPING TO — a budget is hard for many people. The less complicated and formal it is, the easier it is to live with. But it does have to realistically factor in income and expenses.

A disclaimer is in order here: I have never used a formal budget. As a freelance writer, my income is unpredictable, subject to wild gyrations. Yet I usually manage to make ends meet without writing lists of expenses and income. I intuitively adjust my spending priorities as I go along. Admittedly not the best system, but it does work for me—usually. So why do I recommend teaching kids how to budget with a straight face? Because kids do have fairly predictable and uncomplicated sources of income (allowance and jobs) and expenses. Budgeting is easy to learn and implement, and can be a powerful way to acquire discipline.

Linda Kirk Fox, Ph.D., family economics specialist at the University of Idaho Extension, points to two reasons to budget: "To help you live within your financial means, or to help you achieve a particular goal. If earnings are low enough or expenses are high enough, some people have difficulty living within what they make. They can't just go to the grocery store and fill up the basket. If they don't plan ahead they encounter problems."

For kids, a budget can be relevant for achieving a specific goal. You can point out to them that just as athletes and musicians must exercise tremendous discipline to be successful, achieving financial and material goals requires restraint, control, and systemization. Teaching children how to budget will not only help them reach their goals, but will also teach them how to make choices throughout their lives. Chapter 4, "When to Say 'No'," offers techniques for putting kids in charge of a clothes budget to give them practice making trade-offs, and to avoid battles over how much to spend on their sometimes extravagant tastes.

Before helping your kids create a budget, they need to know three things: what percent of their money they think they should devote to saving, spending, and giving away; how much they have at their disposal in a typical week, month, and year; and what they typically have been doing with those funds. The degree of your involvement in filling in the following short tables depends on your child's age and ability to add, subtract, multiply, and divide. At age 6 or 7, you can have them fill in the numbers and you can do the math, explaining it to them as simply as you can as you go along.

Analyzing Income

When kids receive money in dribs and drabs—even on a regular basis—they may not realize that during the course of a month, quarter, or year they actually have some real money. It's easy to let money slip through our fingers in dribs and drabs, too, without realizing that we may be spending quite

TABLE 3.1

Hypothetical Income of a Typical 12-Year Old

	Weekly	× 52	Yearly	÷ 12	Monthly
Allowance	$5.00		$260.00		$21.67
Household chores	$3.00		$156.00		$13.00
Outside jobs (*e.g., babysitting or mowing lawns*)	$10.00		$520.00		$43.33
Cash gifts			$75.00		
TOTAL	$18.00		$1,011.00		$ 78.00

Source: Adapted from material prepared by Lynn White, professor and Extension family economics specialist, the Texas Agricultural Extension Service of the Texas A&M University System.

a lot over time. Decisions about how much to save, and how much and how to spend may change dramatically with this broader perspective.

For instance, I have filled in *Table 3.1* on the previous page to demonstrate how much money a typical 12-year-old may have access to.

Analyzing Outgo

What are your child's habits? Lynn White of Texas A&M University's Extension Service recommends that kids track the outflow of their money for four weeks, as I did in *Table 3.2, below,* for our hypothetical 12-year-old.

TABLE 3.2

Tracking a Month's Expenses

Week	Save For	Share With	Spend For	Total
1	bike $4.00 CD $2.50	church $1.00 food bank $1.00	lunch $8.00 supplies $1.50	$18.00
2	bike $4.00 CD $2.50	church $1.00	lunch $8.00 movie $6.00 popcorn $2.00	$23.50
3	bike $4.00 CD $2.50	church $1.00 Girl Scouts $1.00	lunch $6.40 sports cards $0.75	$15.65
4	bike $4.00 CD $2.50	church $1.00	lunch $8.00 candy $0.75	$16.25
Totals	**$26.00**	**$6.00**	**$41.40**	**$73.40**

Source: Adapted from material prepared by Lynn White, professor and Extension family economics specialist, the Texas Agricultural Extension Service of the Texas A&M University System.

To calculate the annual and monthly averages, we calculate the weekly average by dividing the bottom row of totals by 4, multiply by 52, then divide by 12.

	Weekly	× 52 =	Yearly	÷ 12 =	Monthly
Saving	$ 6.50		$338.00		$28.17
Sharing	$ 1.50		$ 78.00		$ 6.50
Spending	$10.35		$538.20		$44.85
Total	$18.35		$954.20		$79.52

Setting Goals

Once you help your children get their own spending and earning information on paper, you can help them figure out whether they are saving, spending, and sharing enough, too much, or just right (according to their own values and wishes). For instance, our hypothetical teen is saving about 33.5 percent, sharing a tad more than 7.7 percent of her income, and spending a little more than half. Some adults try to target about 10 percent of their own money for charity and like their kids to do the same. Many parents encourage (or force) their kids to save up to one-third of their allowance and earnings. That's great, considering that the earlier they put money into investments or savings accounts, the more their money will earn in compound interest and appreciation (as we discussed in Chapter 2). Considering that recent savings rates for adults have been running a paltry 4 percent, this exercise is usually helpful for parents as well.

As for the spending part of the equation, you can help your kids understand that there are two kinds of spending, notes *Kids, Cash, Plastic and You: A Guidebook for Families on Mastering Money* (put out by the U.S. Office of Consumer Affairs and MasterCard International):

■ Nondiscretionary expenses include necessities such as rent or mortgage, insurance, telephone, heating, and credit-card bills (please see "Giving Kids Credit" for more about credit cards).

■ Discretionary expenses are for extras such as vacations, leisure activities, or new clothes and car.

In the example above, our hypothetical teen shelled out $31.90 on nondiscretionary items (lunch and supplies) and $9.50 on discretionary items (movie, snacks, and sports cards).

Creative Tinkering

The idea of a budget is not to make us feel hopelessly constricted, but to enable us to meet our obligations and dreams. The trick is to build in some flexibility. For instance, our hypothetical teen above spent $7.60 a week less than he or she earned. That comes to $32.93 a month or $395.20 a year! That could be put aside for unexpected, miscellaneous needs or wants.

If, instead, your children find that they are spending *more* than they earn, they are now in a position to make informed decisions. How can they trim expenses? Obviously, the first place to cut back is on the discretionary items. But what are some opportunities for earning more money?

Clinical psychologist Kenneth Kaye says, "What you really need to teach your child is not what to do with his life, his talents, or with his money but how to make choices, so he can make the thousand decisions he will have to make outside your supervision. The only way to do that is to give him real choices to make, freely. If you manipulate him—no matter how subtly—then it isn't really a choice, is it? Your choice may push him into a good experience, but only when he applies that experience to a free choice of his own does he really learn how to be a grown up."

Carol Seefeldt, professor of human development at the University of Maryland, agrees. "I remember shopping with my teenage daughter, and she spent all her money on this awful necklace. I knew she would be sorry, but I let her buy it. She ended up not wearing the necklace. I was able to stay out of her decision, and let her experience that disappointment."

A hint for parents: Avoid the temptation, after the impulse purchase has gathered dust in the child's closet, to say "I told you so." Instead, if the item is something your child is later willing to give away, you can gently revisit what the child spent on it as you write down its value for charitable-deduction purposes.

Giving Kids Credit

ONE 14-YEAR-OLD GIRL posted this on America Online's Parent Soup message board: "I am 14. Like every teen, I ask my mom if I can borrow the credit cards. 'No' is the usual answer . . . DUH! BUT one day I went shopping and I didn't have enough cash, so I went home and asked my mom for the moola for it. She told me since I have been spending MUCH less than usual and she wants to teach me responsibility, she got me a VISA. I was way stoked. I mean I was trippin', totally trippin'. So I went to Target and shopped and shopped and Nordies [Nordstrom's] and GUESS. Then the bill came. Uh oh!!! $1,467.00!!!! I have learned how to manage my money and how much I spend on my mom's cards. If it's something I want, I have to buy it with my own cash. If it's something I need, I charge it. Now my bill has gone way down. I am very scared to pay my own bills when I'm older. But this has taught me a lot lately."

If you think *your* little angel could never, would never, fall prey to the credit demon, consider the following story an extremely thoughtful mother told me about her son:

"I have never bounced a check in over 27 years of marriage, let alone been unable to pay my total card balance each month. I had him earn and save from when he was young. He had worked at Burger King during high school and saved $5,000 toward the $12,000 tuition for his first year at an out-of-state college. We opened up a credit card for him with a $500 line of credit so he would have money for an emergency. I taught my kids to pay off their balance each month, and to use the credit-card money only as a free loan.

"During his first two years he only used the card about five times and for never more than $100. After a while he sent the card back to us because he told us he had gotten his own credit card in his own name. The college had set up sign-up tables all over campus for students to get credit cards. They offered the kids gifts and rewards for bringing their friends to get a credit card. All you had to have was a part-time job and be a student. These credit companies probably felt parents would pay any bills their irresponsible child might ring up. Because my son had such a wonderful credit history, they gave him a $5,000 credit limit! At first he only charged what he could pay with his part-time job. Then he got an internship at a publishing company, and had to work 40 hours a week for no pay. He started to take cash advances on his credit card.

"Then two terrible things happened: He passed out and was hospitalized with a severe case of mononucleosis. My husband's job had been downsized two months earlier so we didn't have medical insurance. My son racked up about $4,000 in medical costs on top of his cash advances on his credit card. Rather than ask us for help he decided to go bankrupt. Now he'll have trouble getting a job because of his credit history, and he will be stamped a loser for 10 years."

Her son may or may not have come down with mono had he not taken the nonpaying internship. I'd argue, though, that he may not have taken the internship and gotten into so much debt if he hadn't been able to live off his credit-card cash advances. Credit cards make it very easy and enticing to live beyond our means for teens as well as adults. From 1992 to 1997, salaries in the United States inched up by about 5 percent a year, while consumer debt blossomed by some 13 percent a year. Not even counting mortgages, Americans now owe more than $1 trillion in revolving credit.

Still, there's a sensible case to be made for letting teens carry a credit card—it's hard to learn how to use one responsibly without having one.

To Co-sign or Not to Co-sign?

When you co-sign a credit-card application, you are responsible to cover the cardholder if he or she gets in over his or her head. But because the bill goes to your kid, you may not know about a problem until it becomes a big one. Two other ways to go: give them an extra card on your own account, so you can monitor their spending each month. Even the 14-year-old girl learned an important lesson after her first binge.

The second option is a secured credit card, with a credit limit up to an amount they deposit in a savings account. The advantage is that the credit limit will be safely low, and interest rates are often lower than unsecured cards. Once they go off to college and are hit with hyped-up offers for credit cards—many come with tempting inducements— with luck they will already have developed some sound spending and charging habits.

Missed or even late payments can blemish one's credit rating for up to seven years and can affect the ability to get a job, rent an apartment, and obtain financing for a car. There are no guarantees that the example you set and the lessons you teach will be effective, but before their first piece of plastic arrives, you would be wise to make sure your kids understand the cold, hard facts. Cardholders armed with information are clearly more likely to use credit wisely, points out Larry Chiang, president of the Oak Brook, Illinois–based United College Marketing Services. He points out that credit-card issuers generally experience a 5.5 percent loss rate among all their cardholder customers, although since the early 1980s, the loss rate has actually been a point lower for college cardholders. Chiang explains that students generally have stable income; they are more responsible than the general public, some of whom may not attend college; students who overcharge do so in the hundreds of dollars, compared with the tendency of some adults to overcharge greater sums. As well, parents may bail out maxed-out kids; adults generally don't have someone to provide a cushion when they get in over their heads.

Chiang boasts that college students who sign up for his company's Visas experience an even lower 2.2 percent loss rate. He attributes this to seminars his company offers on campuses around the country about how to use credit, get your credit report, save money on car loans, and other aspects of personal finance. You can find lots of related information on his Web page (www.collegevisa.com).

Below is information to help you teach your kids how to shop for credit cards, how to set limits on using them, how to plan ahead to repay the debt to avoid becoming overextended, what to do if they do bury themselves in debt, and how to protect themselves against the growing problem of credit-card fraud.

Card Shopping

Interest rates and annual fees are just two of the factors you should guide your kids to consider when they shop for a card. Other variables include inducements such as frequent-flier miles, "discount dollars" on catalog purchases for every dollar charged on a card, rebates, travel and collision insurance on rental cars, and purchase protection (replacement of items charged that are lost, stolen, or broken). These cards tend to be the most expensive, particularly for consumers who use the card infrequently and who consistently pay their balance in full. They will end up paying more in fees and interest for such cards than the value of the perks. In fact, the most important consideration in picking a card is how the cardholder intends to use it.

Revolvers, who maintain a balance month to month, should focus first on interest rates. Most bargain rates are variable, meaning that the issuer will adjust the rate (generally quarterly) in concert with the prime rate (the interest rate banks charge their best borrowing customers) or other rates such as the six-month Treasury bill rate. Some cards advertise very low "teaser" rates that will increase after a period of time. However, even fixed-rate cards are effectively variable because the Truth in Lending Act lets issuers change terms on their credit cards with only 15 days notice.

Transactors, who pay their balance in full each month (only about 25 to 31 percent of all households with credit cards have at least one cardholder who is a transactor), should pay attention to a card's grace period—the number of days between the end of the billing period and the date the interest starts to roll. Not all cards have a grace period. Some begin charging interest on the account's closing day—even before the card owner receives the bill. Cards with a grace period don't charge any interest at all if the card owner pays off the bill in full. When consumers carry a balance, they lose the grace period on all purchases until they pay in full.

Many cards charge an annual fee, which can be $20 to $50 a year, even if the cardholder doesn't charge a single purchase. Many card issuers will reduce or even waive their fees when asked; some may lower their rates. It pays to try to negotiate. Many let the customer trade off between several rate and fee options.

Guide your kids to the disclosure box on the back of credit-card solicitations to find these and the following less obvious costs in the fine print:

Cycles

Some cards use the two-cycle method of calculating interest, which means that as soon as a consumer starts carrying over a balance, the credit-card issuer starts the clock ticking back two months to the date of purchase, not the date of the credit-card statement. For example, if you charged $1,000 on a new two-cycle card in April, your bill arrives in early May and the payment is due near the end of that month. If you pay only part of the bill, then your June bill will charge interest for April and May.

Transaction fees

Some cards charge a fee every time a card is used, others impose fees for exceeding credit limits or paying your bill late.

Where can you find the best rates and features on different credit cards? Every six months the Federal Reserve System (202-452-3000) conducts a survey of financial institutions on the terms of credit-card plans they offer, and publishes the results in its booklet, *Shop: The Card You Pick Can Save You Money.* You can find the results of its most recent survey and the toll-free numbers of credit-card issuers (along with definitions of terms, how to calculate finance charges, and other related information) on-line at www.bog. frb.fed.us/pubs/shop/. Other sources that publish lists of low-cost cards:

- Bank Rate Monitor ($10, 800-327-7717)
- CardTrak by RAM Research ($5, 800-344-7714, or free at its Web site: www.RAMResearch.com/cardtrak/surveys.html)

The Federal Reserve Board's booklet offers some helpful hints about how to find the best deal for your child (or yourself):

- Review all the information about the plans.
- List the desired features that best fit your needs and rank them according to how you plan to use the card.
- Call the institutions you've selected to verify the information and to see if they have any other plans available.
- If you are a current cardholder and have a good credit rating, see if the institution that issued your card will lower your current rate . . . *negotiate.*

Setting Limits

Credit-card–toting consumers are likely to spend more than non-card carriers, so one way to limit the amount you charge is to leave the card home. When your kids head for the mall, suggest they make a list of what they plan to buy and bring enough cash.

When does it make sense to use credit or cash? The National Institute for Consumer Education (NICE) offers the following considerations:

■ How long will I have to save to pay cash? Encourage your kids to hold out and save at least a portion.

■ How long can I wait to have the product? Rosella Bannister, former director of NICE, explains, "There's no hard-and-fast rule, but if you're in Michigan in November thinking about snow boots, maybe you can't wait. If you're in Florida looking for a new swimsuit, maybe you can wait and save up for it."

■ Will the price be higher or lower in the future? "If you're buying a computer, it will probably be cheaper if you

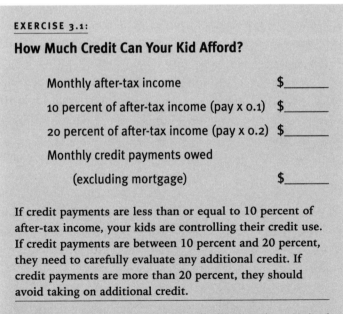

EXERCISE 3.1:

How Much Credit Can Your Kid Afford?

Monthly after-tax income	$_____
10 percent of after-tax income (pay x 0.1)	$_____
20 percent of after-tax income (pay x 0.2)	$_____
Monthly credit payments owed	
(excluding mortgage)	$_____

If credit payments are less than or equal to 10 percent of after-tax income, your kids are controlling their credit use. If credit payments are between 10 percent and 20 percent, they need to carefully evaluate any additional credit. If credit payments are more than 20 percent, they should avoid taking on additional credit.

Source: "How Much Credit Can You Afford?" Fact Sheet, National Institute for Consumer Education, Eastern Michigan University Web site (www.emich.edu/public/coe/nice), 1997

wait," notes Bannister. "If you can wait for several months—for example, if you already have a working machine and are upgrading—not only will the price be lower, but you'll also save on interest and the technology will be less obsolete."

■ Will the convenience or satisfaction I gain from having the product now be worth the interest costs? If not, don't charge.

■ Will the product have value after I have finished paying for it? If not, use cash.

■ Will the monthly payment fit into my spending plan? See *Exercise 3.1* on the previous page to determine whether or not you can afford to charge.

Other ways to set limits is by having your kid apply for a debit, secured, or smart card. Debit cards allow stores, most usually groceries and gas stations, to deduct the amount of purchases immediately from the cardholder's checking account. Some banks charge a fee for each transaction. These cards can also be used at ATM machines.

Secured cards are best for people who might not be eligible for regular credit cards because they have poor or no credit history. The applicant must deposit several hundred dollars with the card issuer, and can only charge up to that amount. These cards are a convenient and safe way for parents to provide money for living expenses to college students. Kids can begin to develop a credit history and get into the habit of charging only up to a preset amount. However, you pay a price for the convenience and security. "They're a horrible deal," says Chiang of United College Marketing Services. "You have to deposit money that pays nominal, if any, interest, and the typical fee is high."

RAMResearch's "CardTrak Secured Card Survey," on-line at www.RAMResearch.com/cardtrak/surveys/secured.html, lists the current offerings of several issuers. The survey doesn't give information about important features such as application fees, the amount of the credit line

TABLE 3.3:

Comparing Secured Credit-Card Offers

	Citizens Bank 800-922-9999	Amalgamated MasterCard 800-365-6464	California Commerce Bank 800-222-1234
Interest rate (percent)	15.65	16.50	17.00
Annual fee	$25	$50	$35
Application fee	0	0	0
Minimum balance	$300	$500	$300
Credit line	100 percent of security deposit	100 percent	100 percent
Grace period	25 days	25 days	5 days
Interest calc. method	Avg. daily balance	Avg. daily balance	Avg. daily balance
Interest on security (percent)	1.73	3.75	2.25

(it's not always the full amount of the security deposit), grace period, or interest calculation method, but you can easily (or, better yet, have your teen) call the 800 numbers, which are listed. *Table 3.3* lists the best deals I found as of June 1998.

Smart cards, also called store-value cards or electronic purses, have a computer chip that tracks everything charged on them. Examples include prepaid phone cards and some transit cards (such as Washington, D.C.'s Metro fare card).

The average household has 10 charge cards, including bank cards and store cards. Most financial experts recommend holding two.

Repayment Plan

The biggest mistake people, old and young, make with credit cards is underestimating the true cost of credit. If your kid makes just the minimum 2.5 percent monthly payment on a $1,000 outstanding balance with 18 percent interest, it would take seven years to repay and cost $730 in interest!

Ideally, you should impress on your kids the importance of writing a check for all their charges each month. If they can't, they should avoid using the card until the balance approaches zero.

Insist that your kids keep track of every credit-card purchase. That means saving all receipts and reviewing monthly statements to make sure they are accurate. United College Marketing Services (800-357-9009) sells a transaction ledger envelope that fits over a credit card. (A set of 12 ledgers can be ordered by sending a $2 check, and your name and address, to UCMS at 2021 Midwest Road, 3rd Floor, Oak Brook, IL 605231.)

Digging Out of Debt

The leading cause of the 1.1 million personal bankruptcies Americans filed in 1996 was credit cards. College kids who take out student loans and get into the habit of maintaining a credit-card balance have the hardest time juggling their finances once they graduate and have to start repaying their debts.

If your high school or college kid gets in over her or his head, there's help. The National Foundation for Consumer Credit (800-388-2227) has 1,300 consumer credit counseling agencies around the country. Their counselors can help negotiate with creditors for lower monthly payments and reduced interest rates, and help maxed-out chargers work out a budget. Late, overlimit, and annual fees, which average $9 a month and range from $5 to $35, can be reduced or even waived in some circumstances.

In 1997 NFCC helped 1.2 million clients, and that number has been growing about 15 percent to 20 percent a year. Only about one-third of these clients had debt problems serious enough to need NFCC's Debt Management Plan, which helped them repay $1.6 billion they owed to banks, retailers, finance companies, and credit unions. Budget counseling helped another third repay their debts on their own, and about 27 percent were given specific assignments to complete before returning for follow-up counseling. Seven percent were referred to an attorney to explore personal bankruptcy as a solution.

Personal Bankruptcy

In 1997, 1.35 million Americans filed for personal bankruptcy, up 14.4 percent from the year before. But this method of digging out of unmanageable debt comes with consequences that no one, much less teens or young adults, finds easy to live with. Before your kids fill out their first credit-card application, you should discuss the fallout from amassing too much debt. You can explain that:

■ Some personal property might have to be sold to repay creditors.

■ Certain debts must still be repaid.

■ Personal bankruptcy stays on filers' records for 10 years, making it almost impossible to open new charge accounts.

■ Renting a car, reserving a hotel room, and even writing checks to many stores (that require a major credit card for identification) becomes difficult.

■ Future employers and landlords, who can legally check applicants' credit record, may not want to hire or rent an apartment to individuals with a seriously blemished credit history.

Protecting Your Kids' Plastic

Cardholders only have to pay up to $50 per account for unauthorized charges made after reporting a lost or stolen card to the issuing bank or institution (the phone number should be listed on the monthly statement). But if several cards are lost or stolen, that can add up.

Here are some tips for protecting your kids' cards drawn from the Federal Reserve Bank of Philadelphia's pamphlet, *Plastic Fraud: Getting a Handle on Debit and Credit Cards* (215-574-6112):

- Safeguard cards as you would cash.
- Separate your cards. Carry with you only those cards you intend to use.
- Never write your personal identification number (PIN) on your debit card; always commit it to memory.
- Never reveal your PIN to anyone.
- Keep your eye on your credit card whenever possible.
- Watch clerks fill in credit-card slips.
- After signing a credit-card slip, ask for the carbons, tear them up, and throw them away.
- Make sure you're handed your own card back, not somebody else's.
- Open your credit-card bills promptly each month.
- Make sure that you made the listed purchases.

If your kids find purchases on their statement that they believe they did not make, they must notify the card issuer in writing within 60 days. Sometimes a phone call resolves the matter, though it's wise to ask for a corrected statement. They don't have to pay for disputed purchases until the problem is resolved.

Another important safety tip: remind your kids not give out your or their credit-card number when they receive a phone solicitation—such callers may not be who they say they are. Cardholders should only give a credit-card number to order things when they initiate the call.

TABLE 3.4

Sources of Credit Information

AUDIOS GEARED JUST FOR YOUNG ADULTS

■ **Smart Credit Card Strategies for College Students,** a 60-minute tape that covers the basics of how to get a first credit card and how to avoid typical mistakes. (Good Advice Press), $15.95, 800-255-0899.

BOOKS TO TURN TO FOR MORE INFORMATION

■ **The Pitfalls of Plastic Credit Cards: A Primer,** by M.M. Tschappat (Pitfalls), $9.95 plus shipping and handling, 303-771-2748.

■ **The Ultimate Credit Handbook,** by Gerri Detweiler (Plume), $12.95.

ORGANIZATIONS TO CALL IF YOUR KIDS GET IN OVER THEIR HEADS

■ **National Foundation for Consumer Credit** (800-388-2227) provides information and counseling to anyone with credit problems.

■ **Debtors' Anonymous** (781-453-2743), a nonprofit, self-help 12-step program for helping debtors achieve solvency (www.debtorsanonymous.org).

Tell your kids to be especially careful with debit cards. If they are lost and the owner fails to notify the bank within two business days, he or she may be liable for up to $500. If notification is not given with 60 days after receiving a statement with unauthorized withdrawals, the cardholder could be responsible for all unauthorized withdrawals.

For a fee, cardholders can list their cards with a card registry, which will notify all your card companies if your cards are lost or stolen. Unless your child (or you!) has many cards, it may make more sense to keep a list of credit- and debit-card numbers, issuers, and phone numbers in a handy and safe place.

Taxes

WHAT VALUES DO we want our kids to have about paying taxes? What are our own values and behaviors? What messages have we been inadvertently giving our children from what they see us do and say?

Three important things to teach our children about taxes is why we pay them, what the government uses our tax money for, and how to do sound tax planning, says Linda Kirk Fox, Ph.D., a family economics specialist at the University of Idaho Extension who created the video, *Enhancing Financial Literacy of Older Youth.* "Don't think of doing tax education only when we file taxes or get a check back, but also when we use the services," suggests Fox. "At the beginning of the school year, talk about who pays for school. What are some other things we use that taxes pay for, such as parks or having the roads snowplowed in the winter? We shouldn't just focus on April 15, because that overemphasizes the negative aspect—the records, math, hassle." You don't want to give the message that all taxes are bad.

Fox says lessons about tax planning should include how to "save money on taxes—not in the context of avoiding them, but as a sound way to handle finances. For instance, you should avoid having too much money withheld just to get a big refund, when you could have had that money working for you all year long."

As of 1998, children under age 18 could earn wage income up to $4,250 tax-free. Above that, they generally pay the lowest bracket of Federal tax, which is 15 percent as of this writing. When children get their first job, they will need to know the difference between gross income and net income. As the pay stub from Your Corner Grocery Store shows in *Illustration 3.1, below,* if they earn $5.70 an hour for 23.75 hours, the regular gross pay is $135.38. But the paycheck will be a bit lower, to reflect money employers take out for federal taxes, state taxes, Social Security (SSI), and Medicare payments. Many employers also withhold disability, medical insurance, and pension contributions. These are called payroll deductions, and whatever is left over after these payments are withheld is called net pay.

Whether or not your children earn enough in active

ILLUSTRATION 3.1:

Your Corner Grocery Store Earning Statement

Jane Doe	Pay Period Ending:	07/30/98
5 Mulberry Street	Hourly Rate:	$5.70
Anytown, Massachusetts	Your Net Pay:	$133.95
SS# 123-45-6789		

DESCRIPTION	CURRENT	YEAR-TO-DATE
Regular hours	23.75	
Total regular hours	23.75	460.25
Regular overtime hours	4.75	
Total overtime hours	4.75	101.75
Gross regular pay	$135.38	$2549.07
Gross overtime pay	40.61	841.65
Total gross pay	175.99	3390.72
Adjusted gross	175.99	3390.72
Social Security withholding	-10.91	-210.22
Medicare withholding	-2.56	-49.17
Federal withholding	-18.90	-295.43
Massachusetts tax	-9.67	-186.31

	ANNUAL	USED
VACATION HOURS	19.00	-
BONUS HOURS	40.00	-

(earned) income or passive (unearned) income to pay income taxes, they do pay sales tax every time they ring up purchases at a store (in most states). When my son quotes the price of something he wants to buy, he tends to forget sales tax. I used to end up coughing up the tax, especially after he has saved long and hard for something he is excited about. What's the big deal? I was missing an opportunity to teach him about an important piece of reality and do some real-world math. So now, as he's saving up for something or as he grabs his wallet on the way to the store, I remind him to add in the tax. He may not love paying more, but he has come to enjoy taking out his calculator and punching in the numbers. The concept is simple enough for most third graders to grasp. The long way is to multiply the price (say, $10) by the tax (0.05 in my state) and then add that to the price:

$$\$10 \times 0.05 = \$0.50$$

$$\$0.5 + \$10 = \$10.50$$

He especially liked learning about the "shortcut" of multiplying the price times 1-point-the tax (in our case, that would be 1.05) to find out the total price:

$$\$10 \times 1.05 = \$10.50$$

Teaching your kids to account for their money won't guarantee they'll become as rich as Bill Gates. But helping them develop good habits early will enable them to go through life more financially responsible and confident with whatever fortunes or debts they amass.

TABLE 3.5

Accountability Tips to Remember

1. Give kids a place to keep their money—ideally, a see-through container that lets them watch their money grow, with an opening that lets them take some out when they want to.

2. Get kids used to keeping track of their money, with computer programs or on paper. Ledgers or unused checking account registers work great.

3. Help kids set up a budget to manage their income and expenses, and to help them meet specific savings goals.

4. Have kids track their income and expenditures for a month, then help them make adjustments (do more chores to earn extra money, or trim some expenses) to make ends meet or save up for special things they want.

5. By age 16 or 17, kids can start to experience using a credit card, either an extra card on your account that lets you monitor their spending, or a secured card (that limits what they can charge to an amount deposited in a special account).

6. When shopping for their first credit card, help them look for features that match the way they will use the card (grace periods for those who plan to pay off each month's bill in full, and low interest rates for those who expect to carry a balance month to month).

7. Negotiate! Especially if you are willing to co-sign on a card for your kids, assuming your own credit history is good, many card issuers will lower interest rates or annual fees, or offer cards that let you trade off lower interest for a fee, or lower or no fees with higher interest.

8. Make sure kids understand that credit is not free; banks earn a lot and consumers pay a lot with credit cards.

9. Encourage kids to keep their charge balances no higher than 10 percent to 20 percent of their monthly, after-tax (net) income.

10. Teach kids to keep track of their credit-card purchases, to save receipts, and to review their statements to ensure purchases they didn't make are not on their bill.

11. To ensure kids have a healthy attitude about taxes, make them aware of government services and benefits (schools, parks, roads, police and fire protection, etc.) that our taxes fund.

12. Once kids get their first outside job, teach them tax planning techniques—how to avoid underwithholding (and the interest and penalties that entails) or overwithholding (letting their money work for them all year long is better than getting a refund check).

13. Show kids how to calculate sales taxes and factor them in when they are saving up for something.

Chapter 4

Guiding Little

Big Spenders

WHATEVER YOUR INCOME BRACKET AND VALUES about things material, it's crucial to help your children learn how to spend wisely. After all, kids have substantial financial resources of their own—$20 billion a year, according to *Business Week* estimates. And that's only for kids under the age of 14. They also exercise lots of influence over some $200 billion of what their parents buy each year.

For all the purchasing power kids have, though, as a group they are not necessarily the wisest shoppers. They are exposed to thousands of commercials during the 25 hours of television the average child watches each week. As well, 8 million–plus kids are exposed to corporate-sponsored teaching aids, such as Channel One, which carry ads for sneakers, soft drinks, and other products. More kids, from single-parent or double-career households, are taking on greater household responsibilities, including grocery and other shopping, at earlier ages, yet many lack basic consumer smarts. Clearly, parents who want to counter the increased influence of marketers who target the youth market face an uphill battle.

Yet we may not always set a good example for our kids. Many of us have acquired expensive tastes and excessive spending habits. "It's important to model good behavior, but if you can't, it's good to cop to your own imperfections," says money psychologist Olivia Mellan, who admits, "I'm an overspender. I don't want my 15-year-old son to be. I can talk to him about my overspending to help him understand that he needs to be different. Left to their own devices, kids tend either to imitate their parents or to rebel and do the opposite. Open discussion is always the answer."

"Unless we teach kids how to manage money, they may not reach their financial goals, regardless of how much money they earn," says Lake Alfred, Florida–based certified financial planner Grady Cash, author of *Conquering the Seven Deadly Money Mistakes* (Financial Literacy Center Publications, 1997). Countless investment guides can help us earn the greatest return on the 4 or 5 percent of our income we save, but what we really need is a *spending* guide to help us make smart decisions with the other 95 to 96 percent of our income—and ways to spend less and invest more. "If you cannot avoid spending mistakes," says Cash, "you won't have any money to invest to make investment mistakes."

Here's what you need to know to prepare your kids for the materialistic world:

- Setting limits on how and how much kids spend
- Countering advertising
- When to say no
- Charitable giving
- Teaching kids how to handle wealth responsibly

TABLE 4.1

Too Much, Too Soon?

A fall/winter 1997 survey of 1,341 kids by Yankelovich
Partners of Norwalk, Connecticut, found that:

76 percent of kids ages 9 to 17 have their own bedroom

59 percent have a TV

55 percent have their own cable/satellite hookups

42 percent have their own phone extension

42 percent have stereo equipment

40 percent have a PC in their home

36 percent have a video game system

29 percent have a magazine subscription

21 percent have a portable CD player

9 percent have a VCR

Source: 1997 Nickelodeon/Yankelovich Youth MONITOR™

- Coping mechanisms during financial setbacks
- Preventing dangerous habits such as gambling and shoplifting
- Deciding when and how to bail kids out of problems

Setting Limits on Kids' Spending

ONE PROBLEM IS WHAT University of Michigan professor Jerald G. Bachman calls "Premature Affluence." His study, updated in 1993, notes, "[In] the absence of payments for rent, utilities, groceries, and the many other necessities routinely provided by parents, the typical student is likely to find that most or all of his/her earnings are available for discretionary spending."

Bachman is concerned that after earning and spending so much discretionary money on their whims, such high school students will experience a decline in their standard of living once they are out on their own and have to foot mundane expenses such as rent. Many have a hard time adjusting to real-world financial demands. Kids with significant sums of discretionary money also are more likely to get involved with alcohol and other drugs, "as well as automobiles which increase mobility, relative isolation from adults, and accompanying risks."

Bachman recommends that parents try to limit working teens' casual spending, charge them some room and board, and perhaps require them to save more than the average teen does for future needs.

The Battle for Your Kids' Brains and Bucks

WHEN MY SON, RYAN, was about 4, he came running to me, breathless with excitement, and described a toy he just saw on a TV commercial. "Guess what, Mom?" he said. "Batteries not included!" Kids are not only impressionable, they are also incapable of evaluating a fast-paced sales pitch with glitzy images and action. A slick ad can convince them a negative feature is really desirable.

Evaluating Ads

Kids need to acquire a healthy skepticism against the barrage of advertisements that seduce young consumers before they're even out of the crib. That's not to say that you should go to extreme measures to shield your children from ads. However, kids do need close parental guidance. The Council of Better Business Bureau's brochure, *Advertising and Your Child* (www.bbb.com/advertising/childad.html) suggests the following tips:

- Explain that advertising is only an "introduction,"

not the whole story. Ads present products only in the best light, emphasizing and sometimes exaggerating positive features. Ads do not reveal negatives.

■ Urge kids to discuss and think critically about what they are seeing.

■ Compare products at home and at the store with a TV ad for that product. Ask your child: "How are they different? Which is more exciting?"

■ Make it real. For instance, if you see an ad showing a child performing tricks on a particular brand of skateboard, ask your child, "If you bought that skateboard, do you think you could do those tricks? How long do you think the kid on TV had to practice before he could do those tricks?"

Three videos poignantly demonstrate many tricks behind TV commercials:

■ *Buy Me That: A Kids' Survival Guide to TV Advertising*, produced by Consumers Union, distributed by Home Vision, $19.95, 800-826-3456.

■ *Buy Me That, Too*, produced by Consumers Union and HBO, distributed by Ambrose Video, $79.95, 800-526-4663.

■ *Buy Me That Three: A Kid's Guide to Food Advertising*, produced by Consumers Union, distributed by Home Vision, $19.95, 800-826-3456.

If your public or school library doesn't own these, you may want to nudge them to add the series to their collection. These videos illustrate tricks TV commercials use to make products look appealing and fun, and show kids talking about their disappointment and frustration when the products turn out not to work the way they expected. A cheaper source of kiddie consumer news and ideas is Consumer Union's bi-monthly magazine, *Zillions* (800-234-2078), currently $16 for a one-year subscription.

Why not have your kids themselves evaluate ads by helping them conduct a product test? Virginia A. Atwood, professor of education at the College of Education at the

University of Kentucky, Lexington, suggests testing the relative quality of several different brands of similar products on durability, safety, and whether directions can be followed easily. She describes such a test with sugarless bubble gum intended for the classroom, but it can also be done at home:

■ Choose several brands of a particular flavor. Help your kids develop a list of three to five variables to test for, such as taste, how long the flavor lasts, smell, how easily bubbles can be blown, and whether the gum sticks to the teeth or face.

■ Outline test procedures. For instance, chew each sample of gum for five minutes before blowing three bubbles, and drink water after each sample.

■ Determine a rating system (*e.g.,* 1=excellent; 2=good; 3=poor).

■ Unwrap samples of each brand and place them in containers marked *A, B,* and *C.* The non-tester keeps track of which brand is in which container. Each tester (your children, a friend or two, and even you!) then tastes a sample from each container.

■ After following the test procedures, each tester should record his or her findings on a summary sheet that will look something like *Exercise 4.1.*

EXERCISE 4.1:

Product Test Summary Sheet

PRODUCT	(1 = great; 2 = so–so; 3 = poor)		
FEATURES	SAMPLE A	SAMPLE B	SAMPLE C
Taste			
How long flavor lasts			
Ease of bubble blowing			
Stickiness to mouth and face			

- Make sure testers keep their opinions to themselves until everyone has finished.
- Tally and graph the results.
- Discuss the results and information shown on the gum wrappers, including weight, nutritional information, price, and unit price. Some questions to consider:

—Should advertisers be forced to tell the whole truth?

—Should it be the responsibility of the consumer, the producer, or the government to decide whether an ad is fair and accurate? Why?

—Can the product be made more cheaply at home? What could be a substitute for the product (such as flavored baking soda instead of toothpaste)?

Comparative Shopping

The lessons from the product test can be applied to shopping trips, during which you discuss with your kids why you are choosing one brand over another and/or encouraging your kids to examine with a skeptical eye things they want to buy.

Say Chelsea has saved up for a new pair of sneakers. She has her eye on a $120 pair of Nikes. When her mom takes her to the mall she spots a perfectly good, but (in Chelsea's opinion) not as cool pair of Converse sneakers for $65—on sale for $40. Her mom can help Chelsea compare each brand using the National Institute for Consumer Education's (NICE) decision grid, which you can find on-line at www.emich.edu/public/coe/nice/compare.html. *Exercise 4.2* on the following page shows how I think Chelsea would have filled out the decision grid.

Here are the steps she takes to evaluate each brand's features.

1. List two or more realistic brand alternatives across the top of the grid.

2. List important product factors down the left side.

3. In the second column, rank each factor by its impor-

EXERCISE 4.2

Decision Grid

	Level of Importance	BRAND A Nike		BRAND B Converse	
	Rank (1–10)	Rating (1–10)	Score rank x rating	Rating (1–10)	Score rank x rating
Feature 1 Comfort	9	9	81	9	81
Feature 2 Design	8	10	80	7	56
Feature 3 Cost *(the higher the price, the lower the score assigned)*	7	2	14	9	63
TOTAL SCORE			175		200

Source: National Institute for Consumer Education, Eastern Michigan University Web site (www.emich.edu/public/coe/nice/compare.html)

tance to her, on a scale of 1 to 10, with 10 being the most important.

4. Divide the column beneath each brand in half, and use the left side to record how she rates each product based on the degree to which each brand supports each factor. Use the same 1 to 10 scale.

5. On the right side of each brand's column, multiply the rank by the rating for each factor and record the score for each factor. Repeat for each brand.

Based only on design, in Chelsea's opinion the Nikes win hands-down, but factoring in comfort and cost, the Converse comes out on top. Even if she ends up going for the Nikes (it is, after all, her money), at least she is learning how to factor features into her decisions, not just emotion. Every trip to the store is a potential lesson. Shel Horowitz, the Northampton, Massachusetts–based author of the self-published *The Penny-Pinching Hedonist: How to Live Like Royalty With a Peasant's Pocketbook* (800-683-WORD, in the United States, or 413-586-2388), suggests letting your kids see you reading labels at the grocery store, comparing prices and ingredients. They will learn that not all brands of cornflakes contain the same amount or types of vitamins, and some may have preservatives or other additives. They will learn that a lower-priced box can cost more per pound than another that weighs more.

If you find Tyler distracting you while you try to read those labels, why not pull him into the activity? Explain what you are doing and let him help you decide. Tell him that unit price helps you compare the cost of products that come in different sizes and types of packages. Generic brands tend to be cheaper, and are often of similar quality to more well-known brands. Explain which generic products you are happy buying and which brand-name products you prefer, and why. By third or fourth grade, when kids can read fairly proficiently, consider sending them down the pet food or yogurt aisle and ask them to choose the healthiest product for the money. If your kids are nagging you to buy them some marshmallow breakfast cereal, challenge them to select a natural kind for under $3.50 a pound.

Horowitz takes his 10-year-old daughter, Alana, and her 5-year-old brother, Rafael, to yard sales. "We don't deny ourselves much. We put a priority on living a high-quality life, but have not found it necessary to spend hundreds of dollars to do it," says Horowitz, whose Web site (www. frugalfun.com) offers plenty of free money-saving and other tips. He finds it's often worth waiting to find something used. "We found a $200 ergonomic typing chair at a tag sale for $10." Horowitz knows when it pays to wait for something new to go on sale. Alana had her eye on a new bike for

$200. Then someone offered her a used one for $100. But Horowitz convinced her she could probably find a new model for that amount. Indeed, they found one on sale for $82. "She knew that when a good one came along we'd buy it for her," says Horowitz.

Conquering Impulse Spending

Impulsive buying is the most common spending problem, according to Grady Cash in his book, *Conquering the Seven Deadly Money Mistakes*. While we all may exhibit this tendency from time to time, Cash points out the following symptoms of those who have a serious problem with impulse buying, and offers these solutions:

Symptoms: Shoppers buy items they don't need and can't afford; lack clear financial priorities; fail to achieve financial dreams because little "must-have" items eat away at any savings they accumulate.

Solutions: Marketing research shows that when shoppers leave the physical presence of the item to "think about it," 90 percent do not return. To get some healthy distance:

- Compare prices in three locations.
- Use a checklist to base shopping on reason, not emotion.
- Carry only enough cash to make planned purchases—don't carry credit cards.
- Put an item on layaway if you simply must give in.

Coupon Clipping

Coupons, especially when used in stores that offer double or triple the face amount off, can save significant amounts of grocery and other bills. Using coupons also demonstrates to your child the value of being frugal. If you hate clipping coupons, perhaps your kids will do it for you. Why not let your child thumb through all those circulars and cut out the products and brands he or she recognizes that you use? As an added incentive, you can even let them keep the savings to buy themselves a treat during your next grocery outing, from a pile of coupons they clip for products they'd like. But be careful. It's easy to get sucked into buying things you otherwise would not. Ten cents off a $2 product you do not need is not a good deal, although the manufacturers might like you to think so.

Evaluating Premiums and Inducements

Has your child ever begged you to buy a particular type of cereal just to get the prize inside? If so, it's time to think about premiums.

The Council of Better Business Bureaus' 1997 *Self-Regulatory Guidelines for Children's Advertising* recommends paying special attention to the use of premiums, promotions, and sweepstakes in advertising to children, to guard against exploiting children, who "have difficulty distinguishing product from premium." You can help your children differentiate products from premiums, and point out any conditions of the premium, which the ad should state in terms that kids can understand. Also discuss how you respond to grown-up premium offers, such as frequent-flier miles for long-distance telephone service, NPR gifts for donations, and $100 checks for switching from MCI to AT&T long-distance phone carriers.

Helping Kids Save Up for Their First Major Capital Expenditures

BUYING A FIRST CAR, home, or any major consumer purchase for your kids can be a generous gesture. It also robs your kids of the pride they would feel if they were to work and save for these things themselves. They are bound to appreciate the value of their material possessions more if they have a hand in earning them.

Even parents who could never afford to help their kids buy such big-ticket items can provide help in other, more important ways. Regardless of which end of the economic spectrum you belong, the longest lasting help you can offer is guidance and emotional, not financial, support. It's the old teaching someone to fish rather than giving them the fish.

An important lesson to teach teens who have saved up for cars is that saving doesn't stop when they make the purchase. Keep those deposits coming! Even if your teen buys the car outright and has no monthly loan payments, she still needs money for gas, insurance, maintenance, and—heaven forbid—costly repairs, notes the National Foundation for Consumer Credit (www.nfcc.org), in its 15-minute teaching guide and video, *Your Ticket to Ride* ($115, 301-589-5600) about teaching teens how to budget, save, and shop for a car.

When to Say "No"

HELPING KIDS BUDGET their money is a great exercise. But what about when it comes to spending your money for things you buy them?

Skokie, Illinois–based psychologist Kenneth Kaye points out, "We don't want our children to do without things others have. It just so happens, though, that refusing to fulfill those demands is our job: saying 'absolutely not' to many things, and 'maybe' to the rest."

Your principles and financial ability or willingness to buy things should be your guide to when to resist opening your wallet. Things on my "absolutely not" list include videogames and toy guns (which my son, Ryan, never developed an urge for anyway). I long-ago banned checkout line candy to avoid the constant battles with him. As Ryan's hobbies and tastes matured, the price tags for things he desires got higher. Like many parents, I have had to deny getting him some things he wanted badly. Sometimes he finds a way to save up. Sometimes he gets practice learning how to accept that he won't get everything his big heart desires.

But no one likes to say "no" constantly. An alternative is to put your kids in charge of buying some things, such as their own necessities. You can sit with your kids to write a list of necessities they have to buy (numbers of jeans, T-shirts, underwear, etc.). Give them a separate clothes allowance, and let them figure out how to allocate the funds. Reward them for finding good deals by letting them keep or spend any leftover cash on other clothes or accessories not on the list.

Nora Fox Handler's seventh-grade son became more conscious of how he dressed last year, but needed help understanding the fickleness of fads. "I now give him a monthly clothes allowance instead of just paying for clothes he won't wear because the fad has changed," says Nora, the Mahomet, Illinois, director of a local school foundation and founder and treasurer of an investment club. "He is learning how to shop for sales and really decide what he wants."

Susan Hahn, who works for America Online's Parent Soup site, has a 15-year-old son who gets a fall and spring clothes allowance (on top of his $10 weekly allowance, of which he must save $2.50). "My husband and I buy big-ticket items like dress clothes, jackets, and shoes. (There's a limit—I'll pay up to $40 for a pair of shoes. If he wants more expensive shoes, he pays the difference.) We also buy his underwear and socks (just to make sure he has them!) and athletic gear. For example, he gets $60 ($12 per T-shirt) for five T-shirts every spring. If he's careful, he can find a couple of plain T-shirts on sale for $7 and then buy himself a couple of nicer, 'label' T-shirts with the extra money."

Kathy Clark, a pediatric nurse in Ann Arbor, Michigan, switched to a similar system when her daughter was 13. "It's amazing how many coats and shoes she needed while I was in charge," she muses. Now her daughter's appetite for clothes has become more reasonable.

I tried this with back-to-school clothes for the first time last year when my son, Ryan, was 9. Before our trip to the mall, we made a list together of the number of long-sleeved pullovers and button-downs, jeans, dressy pants, underwear, and socks he should have. I estimated a reasonable cost for each item and together we calculated the total budget. As long as we came home with the minimum number of each item and didn't exceed the budget, he could pick out what he wanted. With calculator in hand, when he found a couple of pullovers on sale, he was able to apply that savings to buy a silk button-down that caught his eye. Instead of enduring a shopping trip that pitted parent against child, we found ourselves on the same side, collaborating to get the budget to work, and making trade-offs to help him afford the things he wanted.

In any family with more than one kid, the problem of equality and fairness is bound to crop up. "Equality is rarely fair," insists Kaye. "Fairness means consistency between one child and another—except as their different ages, maturity levels, demonstrated responsibility, interests, and needs justify distinguishing between them. [Fair] also means consistency between one time and another—except as the context justifies distinguishing. If you said 'yes' last week and you're saying 'no' today, make clear what your reasons are; show that you're not just being arbitrary."

Kaye says consistency "means that the same criteria be used to make different decisions about different children. It is vital to communicate your reasons to all children and show them that you approach each decision with the same goals and concerns.

"Besides being impractical, equalizing the expenditures on each child would send the very opposite of the message you intended. You want them to feel equally important, equally able to thrive in the world. Focusing too much on dollars is likely to depersonalize your relationship and detract from the separate specialness they feel in your eyes."

Handling Financially Tough Times

S AYING "NO" TO YOUR KIDS is especially painful when financial resources leave you no choice. But you can take some comfort knowing that rocky financial periods hold valuable lessons. "Parents are afraid to have their children getting their feelings hurt," points out Carol Seefeldt, a professor at the University of Maryland's Institute for Child Study. "But children have to experience disappointment. It's part of life, and they learn to adapt and to make wise decisions by experiencing some of this disappointment."

Charles Platten Jr. learned this painful lesson first-hand during a two-year bout of unemployment in the midst of the high jobless rate during the early 1990s recession. The former manager of system design and analysis for a restaurant chain in Springfield, Massachusetts, recalls, "The hardest thing is saying 'no' to your kids. It's one thing when you say 'no' to teach them not to expect too much, and something quite different when you say 'no' because you don't have the money." His entire family shared in the cutbacks, which included restricting eating out (except for special occasions), cutting out buying new clothes except shoes, using coupons for the first time, dropping all the premium cable packages (though keeping the basic channels), and suspending contributions to a private school for a fatherless nephew.

"Giving kids mistaken impressions is not doing them any favor," warns Olivia Mellan, the money psychologist. But that doesn't mean laying everything on the table. "You don't have to tell your 4-year-old that the father is out of work. But you can say daddy's had some changes at work and we all have to be more careful about what we spend."

Handling Wealth

INHERITORS OF SIGNIFICANT WEALTH often feel confused and disempowered by their legacies—at least when they are ill prepared to receive them, says Katherine Gibson, a partner of The Inheritance Project (www.inheritance-project.com). Her Blacksburg, Virginia, nonprofit organization conducts research, mostly by interviewing heirs. Those interviews are the basis of her book, *The Legacy of Inherited Wealth* (Trio Press, 1995, $17.95, 540-953-3977). She insists, "Parents have an obligation to prepare their children financially, emotionally, and socially for the circumstances they'll be in when they inherit money."

Gibson, herself an inheritor, says many parents mistakenly believe they should hide from their kids the fact that the family is wealthy. Avoiding the topic gives kids the message that money is bad and can make them feel guilty for being part of a rich family. "I certainly wouldn't tell a 12-year-old that in 20 years you'll be inheriting $3 million," she says. "It won't mean much to them. But what is important to them is, how does money make them feel in relation to their friends? It's important for parents to tune in to the realm of their [kids'] concerns. It's an ongoing process, not something where you take your son out to lunch and tell him at age 16. You need to build a context to pour numbers and trust information into, so when they actually get 'the news' about how much they're getting and when, it doesn't demolish them." That context includes:

■ Teaching basic financial building blocks (such as those found in Chapter 2 on saving and investing, Chapter 3 on budgeting, and earlier in this chapter on smart consumerism).

■ Exposing kids to children from all different backgrounds besides the country club and private school, and paying attention to their responses and interactions. Gibson adds, "Are they obnoxious, scared, stuck up? How well-prepared are they to be fluid in society up and down the class structure? How compassionate are they? How driven are they by images about what kind of people they are because they have a privileged background?"

■ Modeling a work ethic, but one driven by pleasure in being productive, not by guilt.

■ Modeling and including kids in philanthropic activities, based both on the sense that those with more have a responsibility to share, and that giving should be joyful, not a rote act (please see section on charitable giving below).

■ Recognizing when you don't have the experience, maturity, or competence in any of these areas, and finding other resources to compensate, such as support groups, professionals, peers, or mentors (many of which are listed in the back of Gibson's book). Gibson points out that the older the money gets, the more likely later generations are to be financially clueless. "An entrepreneur will be in a pretty good position to teach financial basics because he or she manages a business and the wealth it generates. But if your father is a third-generation inheritor, he may be flailing through this, too."

Not in Steve Forbes's family. The third-generation publisher of *Forbes* magazine encouraged his five daughters (ages 10 to 24) to learn how to read his magazine and the stock market pages when they turned 10. "Some are more interested, others aren't," he admits. "But they all know the importance of it. It may not be something they'll make a career out of, but they know enough to read the road map."

Forbes recalls the impact of stories about the Depression he heard from his grandfather, founder of the magazine. "The magazine was a roaring success in the 1920s, and was virtually bankrupt by 1932. The idea that things could go up and down were ingrained very early." He tells those stories to his five daughters to help them learn that "there is nothing permanent about success." He also expects his daughters to attend business functions, just as he did, from an early age. "They participate actively in those functions by knowing who is there and what they do. They are expected to converse with guests [mostly top corporate executives], to try to make an environment where we can sell to them. That way they don't take the business for granted."

Keep in mind that the wealthy do not have a monopoly on the issue of spoiling their children. As Skokie, Illinois, psychologist Kenneth Kaye puts it, "It isn't how much money you have that determines how well or poorly your child will do, but how you present those resources to the child and especially how you respond to early warning signs of irresponsibility."

Those warning signs include:

■ Unrealistic or antisocial expectations about what he or she is entitled to.

■ Failure to take commitments seriously.

■ A prevailing sense of materialism, which predominates over other values.

"We don't deny ourselves much," admits Kaye, "so we feel bad about denying things to our children. But no matter how much you spend on the lifestyle of the family as a whole (including your home, vacations, etc.), it is better to be frugal about unconditional gifts—extras, luxuries—to individual children. Consider carefully, when you do want them to have some big-ticket item, whether there are ways to get it to them that inspire responsibility without detracting from its pleasure and value."

For instance, if the kids lobby for a new computer or expensive software game, you might ask them what they are willing to trade off for it. One couple gave their kids the option of going on a planned vacation or installing central air-conditioning in the home. They unanimously chose the cool air. It's also not a bad idea to encourage kids to help save up for out-of-the-ordinary luxuries. The process can be as rewarding as the ultimate purchase: the common goal can strengthen family bonds; the anticipation can help kids experience and appreciate delayed gratification; and once they acquire the item, everyone can share in a sense of pride in the accomplishment.

Preparing your kids to handle wealth involves more than nuts-and-bolts money management, says Dan Rottenberg in *The Inheritor's Handbook: A Definitive Guide for Beneficiaries* (Bloomberg Press, 1998, $19.95). His guide for talking to parents about family-wealth issues can also help parents broach questions about financial and emotional expectations and concerns. For instance, Rottenberg points out, "The biggest obstacles you'll encounter. . .will be emotional matters, not financial ones. Many problems that appear on the surface to be financial—like jockeying for assets or income with your siblings, trustees, and lawyers—actually stem from emotional roots." Understanding this can help you break through many of the challenges you're bound to encounter.

Charitable Giving

MANY PARENTS FEEL that the spirit—and habit—of charitable giving is something they want to instill in their children. Shel Horowitz, the author of *The Penny-Pinching Hedonist,* doesn't scrimp when it comes to philanthropy, but he is very careful about the causes he supports. By making giving a family affair, he not only teaches Alana, 10, and Rafael, 5, to give, but also how to give wisely.

Like many of us, Horowitz receives a fair number of solicitations from charitable organizations. Those supporting causes he disagrees with, he immediately chucks. Those he would like to contribute to, he puts in a file. Every six months, Horowitz, his wife, Dina Friedman, and their kids open the file and decide which organizations to support, and how much of his semiannual donations budget to allot to each. This enables him and his family to make rational and comparative decisions, and ensures that he will meet, but not exceed, his family's giving budget.

The Council of Better Business Bureaus rates some 150 charitable organizations on how well they meet its Standards for Charitable Solicitations, which include whether the organizations disclose their financials and record of giving properly and whether administrative and solicitation costs are below 35 percent of revenue. The CBBB also has a brochure, "Tips On Charitable Giving," that outlines how to evaluate mail appeals, what to do about unwanted mail, and when tax-exempt doesn't mean tax-deductible. Write or call for information at 845 Third Avenue, New York, NY, 10022 (212-533-6200). Or check out its Web site (www.bbb.com).

Here are some other helpful Web sites on philanthropy:

■ The National Charities Information Bureau (www.give.org/) provides a quick reference guide to how well 400 national charities meet its philanthropic standards, tips for wise giving, and on-line ordering of full reports on the charities it evaluates (the first is free, additional reports are $3.50 each).

■ Impact Online (www.impactonline.org/) matches volunteers with nonprofit organizations, including virtual volunteering—activities you can do from the Internet such as technical assistance (on-line research, translating material into another language for a nonprofit agency), and direct contact via e-mail or a chat room (to visit electronically a homebound person, provide on-line mentoring, help students with homework).

■ Internet Nonprofit Center (www.nonprofits.org/) contains a library of publications and data about nonprofit organizations, a nonprofit locator to help find any charity in the United States, a chat room, and bulletin boards.

■ Who Cares (www.whocares.org/) publishes a

national quarterly journal devoted to community service and social activism, challenging readers to consider new ways of fixing society's problems. You can get a free full-year trial subscription by calling 800-628-1692.

Don't forget you can make volunteering time a part of your charitable campaign. Craig Aronoff, a professor of management at Kennessaw State University in Marrietta, Georgia, bases decisions about where to donate money on where his two teenage daughters volunteer their time. Collecting food for the survival center, working at a soup kitchen, and visiting the local nursing home are just some ways you can spend quality time with your children, do some good for the community, raise your kids' awareness of people less fortunate, and demonstrate ways they can make a difference.

Gambling, Betting, Lottery Tickets, and Other Bad Habits

EDWARD LOONEY CALLS IT the "hidden epidemic." The executive director of the Council on Compulsive Gambling of New Jersey (CCGNJ) says that compulsive gambling is an even bigger problem for adolescents (about 12.5 percent of whom are affected in his state, home of Atlantic City) than adults (for whom 2 to 8 percent have a serious problem nationwide). In a CCGNJ 1991 survey of 3,000 students at 50 high schools, almost 90 percent said they had gambled within the past year and nearly one-third admitted they gambled at least once a week. Some 2 million U.S. teens are compulsive gamblers, according to clinical psychologist Durand Jacobs, clinical professor at Loma Linda University Medical School and first vice president of the National Council on Problem Gambling.

Looney says that on college campuses, it has hit epidemic proportions.

Gambling is so ingrained in our society, and seems so

benign, that it's difficult to see as a serious threat. Many kids see their parents buying lottery tickets or taking off for a weekend in Atlantic City or Las Vegas. Forms of gambling are even sanctioned by some of our most respected institutions, including churches and synagogues, schools, and our governments, which sponsor lotteries, bingo, raffles, and casino nights to raise funds for socially lofty causes. In fact, Looney recalls learning about an academic incentive program called a "betting board" that a local teacher was using. Students bet they will get an 80 or 90 on an exam, and if they "win," they get a soda or other reward. "What that teacher didn't realize was that this is a vulnerable time. Kids start gambling for money as early as 10 or 11 in inner cities, and 12 to 13 in the suburbs." The average age at which adult compulsive gamblers started betting is 14.

What's the big deal? For those who hit the third stage—the desperation phase (after the winning/action and losing phases)—other serious problems are likely to surface, including stealing, drug dealing, and even prostitution. Jacobs reports that teens with serious gambling problems were twice as likely to attempt suicide (12 percent) as their classmates (6 percent).

Kids often start betting with seemingly harmless games. One popular high school dice game, called see-lows, is not obviously gambling, because it is often played "as is"—no money changes hands during the game. At the end of the week, though, the kids tally their wins and losses, which can run into hundreds of dollars. High schoolers often graduate to sports betting, with sports tickets. For a buck, your teen can buy a ticket (typically from a classmate "bookie" who gets commissions on his "customers'" losses, often to pay off her or his own gambling debt). If you pick three teams that win, you get $8 back; four winners will yield $11. Sounds enticing, but Looney points out, "It's a sucker's bet. The bets are based on point spreads. It's hard to win." Kids who don't win can rack up big losses, which is where the other problems start to kick in.

Looney describes one 16-year-old boy who owed $3,000 to his bookie. Not able to pay, he started booking his own customers, earning 50 percent of their losses—which the bookies are held responsible for. When one customer couldn't pay his own debt, the 16-year-old bookie was driven by his "employer" at night 10 miles to a dangerous inner city block as a warning. After walking home alone, frightened, he told his parents. They called the prosecutor and police, who pursued a major investigation. That story had a happy ending, but many do not.

If you think your teen is so popular, active, and outgoing that she'd never get caught up in such a situation, think again. Those are the very traits that fit the profile of adolescent compulsive gamblers, at least in the early stages. Teen gamblers come from all social backgrounds and are both male and female. The CCGC points out these warning signs for parents to watch for:

- Unexplained need for money
- Money or valuables missing from your home
- Weekly or daily card game in youngster's room
- Truancy from school
- Unusual time spent watching sports on TV
- Unusual interest in newspapers, magazines, and periodicals that have to do with sports or horse racing
- Large amounts of money in his/her possession
- Sudden drop in grades
- Gambling language in his conversation (*e.g.,* 5 timer, 10 timer, bookie, loan shark, point spread, underdog, or favorite)
- Boasting about winnings
- Unaccountable explanation for new items of value in their possession (*e.g.,* jewelry or clothes)
- Several calls on your phone bill to a 900-number sports phone, which announces up-to-the-minute scores of major athletic games

■ Change of personality (*e.g.*, irritability, impatience, criticism, or sarcasm)

■ Unaccountable time away from home

In 1994 alone, some 143,000 youngsters were caught trying to sneak into Atlantic City casinos, and another 10,815 were caught inside. Five casinos were convicted of allowing minors as young as 14 to gamble on their premises.

What to do if you suspect your children may have a gambling problem? Although this is one of the most difficult addictions to spot, it is one of the most treatable—once parent and child acknowledge there is a problem. However, many parents tend to be in more denial than their teens. Gamblers Anonymous, based in Los Angeles (213-386-8789) can refer you to local 12-step programs, many of which sponsor groups for youth. The CCGNJ's Web page (www.800gambler.org) has more than 100 pages of information. School counselors or chemical dependency counselors at school can provide private counseling or refer you to other resources.

Shoplifting

SHOPLIFTERS ALTERNATIVE, an educational rehabilitative home-study program and referral network, *not* a 12-step program (a division of Shoplifters Anonymous), estimates that 23 million people steal from retail stores each year. The National Retail Security Survey says that costs retailers some $8 billion in losses a year. If caught, shoplifters may face a fine, community service, probation, and a jail term. Yet an estimated 25 percent of offenders continue to shoplift.

Most shoplifters are not otherwise criminals. Many have no idea about how or why they pilfer. Peter Berlin, executive director of Shoplifters Anonymous, believes kids do it to relieve anxiety. "While teens, like adults, usually know the difference between right and wrong," he writes in an article, "Why Do Shoplifters Steal?" on SA's Web site (www.shopliftersanonymous.org/), "when their life becomes too stressful they become more vulnerable to temptation, peer pressure, and other things that can lead them to shoplift." He says shoplifters often harbor many misunderstandings:

- They don't think anyone really gets hurt.
- They think the stores can afford the losses.
- They think they won't get caught.
- They don't understand the consequences to themselves and their future.

■ They don't know how to handle temptation when they want nice things, or feel pressured by friends, or are mad at the world and want to strike back.

■ They don't know how to resolve feelings of anger, frustration, depression, unattractiveness, or unacceptance.

Tough life situations may not easily be changed, but shoplifters' coping mechanisms can. Shoplifters Alternative's education programs (including a $56 cassette home-study course) help offenders understand how shoplifting affects the lives of real people (not just stores); the law and its consequences; new security technology now used in stores to detect shoplifters; how much they risk for a small reward; and how shoplifting can become addictive. Shoplifters Alternative also tries to help shoplifters see how their own personal and social pressures can trigger a shoplifting incident and it teaches them how to put shoplifting behind them.

The National Report on Shoplifting, published by Shoplifters Alternative, claims that educating shoplifters both about the problem and about themselves is extremely effective, bringing recidivism down from 25 percent to 1.5 to 3 percent.

But don't ignore your own role. What messages have

> **TABLE 4.2**
>
> ## Who Steals What, When?
>
> ■ Males account for 55 percent of apprehended shoplifters.
>
> ■ 45 percent are females, but they steal more per incident.
>
> ■ About 40 percent of all apprehended shoplifters are younger than 18.
>
> ■ Almost 33 percent are age 13 to 17, although this age group represents only about 7 percent of the U.S. population.
>
> ■ Teens tend to steal things that they either can't afford or are prohibited from buying, such as recorded music, cosmetics, stylish apparel, tobacco products, and consumer electronics.
>
> ■ The average amount of theft per incident is $56.67.
>
> ■ Thefts take place anytime, with "amateur hour" occurring on the weekends, when about one-third of offenders are apprehended.
>
> *Source:* National Retail Security Survey, conducted by Loss Prevention Specialist, Winter Park, Florida

you been modeling to your children about honesty? Do you claim they are younger than they are so you can take advantage of lower kiddie prices at movies, restaurants, etc.? Do you claim personal expenses as business expenses on company expense accounts or income-tax returns? Kids pick up on such behavior and use it to justify their own.

In addition to criminal prosecution, most states also have laws that allow retailers to demand and collect financial damages from adult or juvenile shoplifters as a civil cause of action. The civil damages help retailers offset losses and added costs for security. They also act as a deterrent for offenders, especially young ones, whose parents tend to take their child's shoplifting behavior more seriously when they have to shell out $100 to $500. Some retailers agree to reduce civil damages if the shoplifter agrees to enroll in and successfully complete an SA rehabilitation program.

For more information on Shoplifters Alternative or to reach its toll-free hotline, call 800-848-9595.

When to Bail Kids Out

IF KIDS GET INTO TROUBLE for shoplifting or breaking a neighbor's window, letting them take responsibility is a powerful lesson. But there are times when you may want to consider stepping in.

M. Melinda Tschappat, a former banker, co-authored *The Pitfalls of Plastic Credit Cards* with her son, Scott Douglas Tschappat, after she lent him—and her daughter—cash to help get them out of significant credit-card balances they had amassed during college and in their early 20s. She says she pitched in for three reasons:

"One, I had the funds to help them, even though it hurt my own financial plan. Two, I did not want my children to go through the agony of bankruptcy. They are bright, thoughtful, responsible, and educated; children who would make any mother proud. Their mistake was not coming to me sooner. Three, I realized that somewhere along the way I had not done an adequate job of educating them to the pitfalls and the correct use of credit cards."

But her bailout was contingent on their signing a financial agreement that stipulated the terms of a contract, including a low interest rate. She reports, "My daughter has finished paying her debt, and my son is in the painful process of paying. Would I lend them money again for debt purposes? No. Now their financial future is up to them."

TABLE 4.3

Spending Tips to Remember

1. Model good spending habits.

2. If you can't model good spending, talk to your children honestly about the issue.

3. Help teens who earn significant money learn that not all money is discretionary—by charging them room and board and/or requiring them to increase the amount they save.

4. Teach kids when they are young a healthy skepticism about advertisements.

5. Consider doing product tests at home with different brands of the same item and compare their findings to claims of ads for those products.

6. Encourage children to examine several brands of things they want to buy, and to compare unit pricing before making the purchase.

7. Make every trip to the store a potential lesson by verbalizing how you weigh information on labels of different products as you read them.

8. When kids get restless on shopping trips, pull them into the activity by challenging them to find (or help you find, for younger kids) products that meet your criteria.

9. Show your kids you can wait to buy things for yourself until you find a better deal.

10. Conquer impulse spending by encouraging kids (and yourself) to compare prices in at least three locations, buying only what's on shopping lists prepared in advance, and carrying only enough cash to make planned purchases.

11. Use coupons, but only for products you would normally buy.

12. Teach your kids how to start a budget by tracking their income and expenses for several weeks, especially when they need help saving up for something specific.

13. Explain the difference between discretionary and nondiscretionary income (as we discussed in Chapter 3 in the "Budgeting" section).

14. Let kids make mistakes. It's better to buy a relatively inexpensive piece of junk now than a high-ticket piece of junk when they are older.

15. Remember that it's your job to say "no."

16. But to avoid always saying "no," put kids in charge of buying their own clothes and sundries within a budget, so they learn to make trade-offs. Let them keep money left over to encourage them to find good deals.

17. With siblings, remember that strictly equal is not necessarily fair. Use consistent criteria for making decisions, yes, but don't feel each kid needs to have everything the other has.

18. Consider being upfront with kids during financial setbacks, and include them in finding ways to cut back.

19. Be honest with kids in age-appropriate ways about family wealth and prepare them to handle it.

20. Include children in your charitable giving decisions by having them help you identify causes you agree with and comparing the efficiencies of different organizations that support each cause.

21. Don't forget that volunteering time is an important part of charitable giving.

22. Be alert for signs that your kids might have problems with spending, gambling, or shoplifting, and get immediate help from community and professional resources.

PART 2

Sprouting Financial Wings

How to launch your kids into

the world and equip them

to live financially independent

and productive lives

Chapter 5

Getting Your Child

To and Through

College

WHEN IT COMES TO FINANCING YOUR KIDS' college education, there are two important rules of thumb. First, it's never too late. Even if your child is in her senior year of high school and you haven't saved a penny, you are likely, if you know what you're doing, to find some combination of savings, loans, grants, scholarships, and work-study programs to help you and your child bear most of the financial burden. Also keep in mind that despite the frightening projections about escalating costs, according to the College Board, only 4.3 percent of undergraduates actually pay $20,000 or more per year for college expenses; the majority of students pay less than $6,000 per year.

The second rule is that it's also never too early to start

college financial planning. The sooner you start, the more your money will work for you. Discount brokerage firm Charles Schwab points out that for every five years you delay investing, you may need to *double* the amount you set aside each month to reach the same goal. Unfortunately, many parents don't save at all for their children's higher education. A recent *Money* magazine poll found that 87 percent of U.S. parents expect their kids to attend college, but 47 percent of them have yet to start setting aside funds for their kids' tuition.

Financing tuition is only one of several important issues you face in preparing yourself and your child for college. You also need to become a savvy shopper for the right school. And before teens become college freshmen, it is wise to prepare them for managing their own living expenses.

The more you involve your kids in all aspects of the process, the more prepared your kids will be not only for college, but for their first experience in independent living. In fact, fight any tendency you might have to assume control. "The whole process of selecting the most appropriate postsecondary opportunity is the students' responsibility first and foremost, but they can't do it alone," says James Montague, director for guidance and counseling services at the College Board's New England Regional Office in Waltham, Massachusetts. "Parents, counselors, and other significant adults should play a role but not take over. It's hard for parents to step back and play a supportive, not decision-making role."

The College Board suggests that you kick off the process by initiating a conversation about what your teen wants to learn. Even if he has yet to identify a clear career path, you should discuss where to start: with liberal arts, perhaps. Next outline what kind of help you are willing and able to offer, and what sacrifices you each can make. As early as middle school, your kids will benefit from learning what different colleges will cost, how much of those costs they can count on you to cover, and how much of their own savings you (and financial aid formulas) expect them to chip in.

Saving without Losing Your Sanity

YOU AND YOUR CHILDREN will need to base each of your savings goals on an estimate of how much college will cost by the time your kids pack their bags. By the time my 10-year-old son gets to college in 2006, if tuition continues to rise 5 percent a year, it could cost about $62,481 for four years at a public school, or $126,612 for a private school. The younger your children, and the more years away college is, the less reliable those inflation assumptions are bound to be. Who would have predicted double-digit inflation in the late 1970s? Who would have known that today college costs are rising faster than inflation (5 percent versus 3 percent)?

Pinning down future inflation is not your only challenge. Calculating how much you need to save requires you to make other questionable assumptions—such as how much interest you expect your money to earn. To be on the safe side, you may decide to underestimate future interest rates. But then your calculations could turn out to require a higher monthly investment than you can afford. Many parents are so intimidated by either the uncertainty or the high savings numbers that they end up ignoring the whole issue, and save little or nothing. They limit future financial options for themselves and their children.

Robert A. Ortalda, a consulting chief financial officer in Redwood City, California, has an intriguing alternative. Ortalda, the author of *How to Live Within Your Means and Still Finance Your Dreams* (Simon & Schuster, 1990), has a funding program that doesn't require you to project or even factor in future inflation or interest rates. Ortalda's formula also guides you to set aside less in the early years, and more in the later years when your earning power is likely to be greater. The trick, he says, is to "always assume you're trying to buy something at today's current price. Then assume that your money is not going to earn 8 or 12 percent, but the historical 2 or 3 percent real return (interest rates minus inflation)." He explains, "You'll actually be more on target than if you tried to predict inflation and returns on your investment."

Ortalda's formula may be too complicated to figure out with most pre-high-school kids, but once they hit the teen years you may want to challenge them to help you run

TABLE 5.1

How Inflation Shrinks Your Growing Savings

Nominal interest rates, which averaged about 8 percent for the years shown, have gyrated from more than 11 points from high to low, while inflation averaged 5 percent with a variation of 8.5 points. The real interest rate (nominal interest minus inflation) averaged just over 3 percent and fluctuated in a narrower range of 7 points.

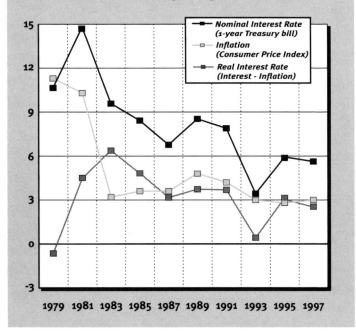

through the calculations. Their involvement will hone their math skills, help them understand and appreciate the financial realities, and model the habit of thoughtful financial planning.

Here's how Ortalda's funding system works. Say your child will be going to college in 10 years and you have saved nothing. According to the College Board, the 1997–98 estimated average total expenses (including tuition, fees, books, room, and board) come to $10,069 for public schools ($21,424 for private schools). Four years of public college therefore costs $40,276 in today's dollars (remember, we're ignoring price increases). However, as a rule of thumb, most parents can plan to cover only about one-third of the cost from savings—the rest comes from various forms of financial aid. In this case, one-third comes to $13,425. Using Fidelity's on-line calculator (personal11.fidelity.com/toolbox/college/calculator.html), I figure that over 10 years, assuming a real interest rate of 2 percent (and 0 percent inflation), you would have to save $1,226 per year, or $102 and change per month.

Instead of using the on-line calculator, you can figure out how much to save per month with *Table 5.2*, which lists the required monthly payment to fund $1,000 in today's dollars assuming different interest rates. For the example above, to fund $13,425 in 10 years at an assumed real interest rate of 2 percent, you would multiply 13.425 (for each $1,000) × 7.53, which comes to $101.09.

Ortalda's scheme is a great way to keep up with tuition costs, which will increase over time. Just recalculate actual costs every year or two. In two years, say actual college costs rise about 5 percent a year (the average rate of increase over the past 10 years), to $10,572, or $42,288 for the full four years. Remember, you only plan to fund one-third, or $14,096. Subtract from that the amount you've amassed over the first two years at the actual rate of return you earned (about 15 percent if you were in the stock market the last couple of years)—about $3,026. The result: Your new funding goal is $11,070 in eight years. Using *Table 5.2, right,* and assuming the same real interest rate of 2 percent, you now need to set aside 11.070 × 9.61, which comes to about $106.38 a month.

Ortalda adds, "We recalibrate everything based on actual inflation of the object you're buying, not an artificial statistic like projected inflation. My system tracks actual market forces like a gun sight follows a moving target. You don't have to know the rate of future inflation or even understand how inflation works."

Another advantage of Ortalda's funding program over most savings programs is that it allows you to save a little more each year as your income rises. Most funding programs have you save level amounts each year. Typically, however, you earn less in earlier years and have more pressures when you are a younger family. Ortalda explains that just makes it harder for many families to commit to funding. "In trying to deal with the reality of undersaving, it doesn't make sense to aggravate the problem by front-loading the cost of funding."

Even if you cannot afford the amount you estimate you need to save, save however much you can—and encourage your kids to do the same. At least that amount will compound over the years and you will have more options later than if you do nothing now. Before you decide how much or little you can afford to set aside, though, consider one client of financial planner Grady Cash, founder of the Center for Financial Well Being in Lake Alfred, Florida.

The family had below-median income, with two children and one on the way. They lived in a small home in the poor part of town, and called Cash to help them start a college fund for their children. "Sitting at their second-hand kitchen table," says Cash, who also wrote *Conquering the Seven Deadly Money Mistakes* (Financial Literacy Center Publications, 1977), "I asked them how much they could afford to save. The husband said, 'Well I think we might be

TABLE 5.2

Required Monthly Payment to Fund $1,000

Years Until College	ANNUAL INTEREST RATE*					
	2 percent	3 percent	4 percent	6 percent	8 percent	10 percent
2	$40.87	$40.48	$40.09	$39.32	$38.56	$37.81
3	26.98	26.58	26.19	25.42	24.67	23.93
4	20.03	19.63	19.25	18.49	17.75	17.03
5	15.86	15.47	15.08	14.33	13.61	12.91
6	13.08	12.69	12.31	11.57	10.87	10.19
7	11.10	10.71	10.34	9.61	8.92	8.27
8	9.61	9.23	8.86	8.14	7.47	6.84
9	8.46	8.08	7.71	7.01	6.35	5.75
10	7.53	7.16	6.79	6.10	5.47	4.88
15	4.77	4.41	4.06	3.44	2.89	2.41
20	3.39	3.05	2.73	2.16	1.70	1.32

* Assumes monthly compounding of interest
Source: Robert Ortalda

able to save $200 a month.'" If they can commit to that much, many others in higher income brackets should reevaluate their goals as well as their values, insists Cash.

"Many people profess the goal is saving for their kids' college education, but say 'we don't have money' and that's where it stops," he says. "Sometimes the goals provide motivation, and sometimes they don't." Cash believes that where goal-based saving may fail, values-based saving is more likely to succeed. "If you're honest about identifying your values, then the values provide the motivation."

Some parents rationalize that saving for college means they will get less financial aid. That's not entirely accurate. Financial aid calculations give more weight to income than assets. Parents are expected to contribute up to 47 percent of their available income toward tuition, but only about 5.65 percent of their savings. There's no way around it: The earlier and more you and your children save, the easier it will be for you and them in the long run.

Almost Painless Ways to Start Saving Early

The single most important action is to start saving early and regularly. Consider setting up an automatic savings plan through a bank or mutual fund. Parents should suggest that their teens, if they have a job, do the same. Even younger kids may want to sock away at least 10 percent of their allowance and other sources of income, which you can encourage by offering to match what they deposit in a savings account.

Unless you are the extremely nervous type, plunk most college savings during the early years into equities, which historically offer higher returns than other investments. Don't try to time purchases with downturns or lock in a profit during peaks. As we mentioned in Chapter 2, dollar-cost-averaging investors—people who buy a set dollar amount of shares in stocks or mutual funds each month, regardless of market gyrations—generally outperform market-timers. Ignore day-to-day gyrations. You are investing for the long term.

Redirect former payments and extra income

Whenever you get extra money, such as a bonus or tax refund, earmark it for college saving. Your kids can devote a percent of their own windfalls, such as cash birthday gifts, to their savings account. Divert payments and expenses you finish making for a car, or for a personal loan, or for things like diapers, formula, and day care. Keep making such payments, but to your college fund instead.

Keep a separate account for college funds

Lynne Goldberg, senior vice president for marketing at Fidelity Investments' Mutual Fund Group, says, "You'll be less likely to dip into college savings for other things you might be tempted to buy if you segregate that money." You can keep one college fund for all your children. Kids, too, should separate college savings into an "untouchable" account.

Have fun getting everyone involved

Goldberg suggests asking grandparents and other relatives to give gifts in the form of contributions to college.

Prepay tuition at today's cost

Some 23 states allow residents to pay now close to current rates for four years' tuition at a state college for their young children. Many offer different payment options, such as shelling out the lump sum when you sign up, depositing monthly payments for five years, or making monthly payments from anytime after birth through the end of high school. The main benefit is that regardless of how much costs may rise, you don't have to contribute another penny for tuition, which has escalated an average of 8.7 percent a year for the past 15 years, and as mentioned earlier, is currently rising about 5 percent a year according to the College Board. The plans typically offer higher interest than certificates of deposit or savings accounts. You might come out ahead by investing the same money in the stock market or in mutual funds. However, prepaid tuition plans are exempt from state and local taxes. They are subject to federal income tax, but at the child's rate, and not until the child matriculates.

A major disadvantage is that prepaid plans reduce federal financial aid eligibility dollar for dollar. Other assets held in the parents' name (except pension funds and home equity, which are not counted at all) only reduce financial aid eligibility up to 5.65 percent. Even assets held in the child's name reduce eligibility by only 35 percent.

Other important considerations: What if the college goes out of business? What if you move to another state? What if your child is not admitted or does not want to attend that school? If your child decides to go to a private or out-of-state public school, you may only get a refund for the original amount you prefunded, possibly with little or no interest. Some states offer more flexibility, allowing you to apply the value of your prepayments to other institutions around the country (for a modest processing fee of $25 to $50 per semester).

For instance, Jon McLaughlin, a construction manager in Virginia, has $200 a month automatically deducted from his checking account to prepay tuition for his 7½-year-old daughter, Tess, who lives with her mother in upstate New York. Virginia and New York have a reciprocal agreement that will allow Tess to attend any public college in either state.

FinAid's Web site (www.finaid.com) provides details about the terms of each state prepaid plan and how to contact them.

Where to invest

There's no one best type of college investment for all people. Your time horizon and personal comfort should be your guide to how much risk you should assume. It's one thing to invest in high-risk international equity mutual funds, growth mutual funds, common stocks of small companies, or even high-yield (junk) bond mutual funds in the very early years. But these are not wise choices when there are only a few years until college, and a collapse in the price of any of these investments might not have time to rebound. You don't want to end up having to sell some of your holdings at a loss when the first tuition bill arrives. Historically, the stock market has offered the highest long-term returns—much higher than more conservative, fixed-rate investments such as CDs. In the short run, though, if the market takes a dip or (gasp!) a dive just when you need to liquidate some of your portfolio for tuition, you might be caught short. So up until college is about five years away, your best bet is generally to invest in equities. The safest and least expensive way to do that is through no-load mutual funds (described in Chapter 2).

Diversify, diversify, diversify! Mutual funds automatically achieve this, but it may also pay to invest in several growth-oriented mutual funds. Many mutual fund companies offer special college investment programs that waive or reduce fees and lower minimum investment criteria. For instance, Fidelity's program allows parents to open an account with a minimum amount of $1,000 instead of its usual $2,500 requirement. If parents don't have even that much, they can open a $100-a-month direct-deposit money market account with the option of switching to its college savings program once the account balance reaches $1,000 (less than a year). It also waives load fees on its Blue-Chip Growth Fund for college savers. Two mutual funds directed at children have even lower minimum investment requirements on custodial accounts: USAA's First Start Fund can be opened with as little as $250 or a $20 monthly automatic investment; Stein Roe's Young Investor Fund requires $1,000 or a monthly $50 deposit plan (please see section on mutual funds in Chapter 2 for details).

You can keep a portion of your college portfolio in safe U.S. Series EE savings bonds. Investors don't have to pay tax on the interest on EEs until they redeem the bonds. Kids usually have a lower tax bracket, so it may make sense to register EEs in their name (see next section, "In Whose Name Should You Save?" for details). However, EEs used to pay for college are exempt from federal income tax on the interest if the bonds were issued in 1990 or later, in one or both of the parents' names (not the child's), and married parents file joint income tax returns. Also, the owner must be at least 24 before the bond was issued, and the bonds must not be redeemed until the year they will be used to pay for college tuition and fees (but not for room and board).

EEs can be purchased in denominations as small as $50 face value (that cost $25). EE bonds issued after May 1, 1997 pay 90 percent of the rate on five-year Treasury bills, which put EE interest rates at about 5.6 percent as of early 1998.

Bonds bought April through December 1993 will take less than 18 years to reach face value and pay at least 4 percent interest, compounded semiannually. Bonds bought between 1991 and March 1993 are guaranteed to reach face value in less than 12 years and pay at least 6 percent interest, compounded semiannually.

America Online's MoneyWhiz site lets you download free shareware that can calculate the current value of EEs (you need the Excel spreadsheet software to use it). To find it, AOL subscribers should use keyword: MoneyWhiz. First double-click "Saving & Investing" and then "Download: Investment Software."

At your child's 10th birthday, you should gradually transfer your portfolio into lower-risk securities, such as investment-grade corporate and insured municipal bonds, and unit trusts of these bonds held to maturity. Until your child is 13, you can also dabble in moderate-risk investments such as common stocks of major companies with good earnings and dividend performance records, investment-grade corporate bond mutual funds, and government securities mutual funds. When your adolescent turns 15, it's time to concentrate more of the college savings on no-risk alternatives such as bank certificates of deposit, money market accounts, savings accounts, Treasury bills, and U.S. government bonds (zero bonds if held to maturity).

In Whose Name Should You Save?

Many experts recommend that you keep college savings in your account. It prevents the kids from blowing those funds on something other than college, such as a trip abroad or a fancy car. You may be tempted to keep the money in the children's names because interest and appreciation would be subject to their lower income-tax rates. But if you even remotely expect to apply for financial aid, keeping the money in your name ends up being much less expensive. Many people who earn comfortable salaries are surprised to learn that they are eligible for some financial aid.

Federal financial aid formulas (which most colleges follow) require that 35 percent of the student's assets be used for tuition, but only 5.65 percent of the parents' assets—not much more than the interest you would earn if those assets were in a money market account.

You may be able to have at least a slice of the cake and eat it, too. If you plan to seek financial aid and you calculate you would have to contribute less with the money held in your name—but want to take advantage of your kid's lower tax rate—keep the money in your kid's name until at least one year before your child plans to enroll. Then transfer all college savings to your name.

If you put the money in your kid's name, you can maintain some control by putting it in a trust or in a custodial account. Setting up a trust requires the services of a lawyer experienced in estate planning. A trust is therefore more expensive to create and maintain than a custodial account, but may still be a good choice if you are setting aside a significant sum. The type of custodial account you can set up—the Uniform Gifts to Minors Act (UGMA) or the expanded Uniform Transfers to Minors Act (which allows transfers of any type of property)—depends on the state in which you reside.

Procrastinators' Alert

Eeeeek!! What if you haven't saved anything and college is only a few years (or less) away? You and your kids have several ways to reduce the financial burden. Parents can borrow from a pension or take out a home-equity loan; high-school kids can earn college credit, plan to spend the first two years at a less expensive community college, and take a job to help cover expenses.

Borrow from your pension

Pensions such as IRAs and company salary-deferral 401(k) plans are not counted in financial aid formulas, so no matter how much you have socked away in your pension, your child still may qualify for need-based grants or scholarships. In fact, if you can only afford to contribute to one account, contribute to your tax-advantaged pension instead of a taxable college fund or other savings account.

Tom Sale, financial services specialist for Olympus America in Chicago, is banking on his 401(k) to cover some college costs. He's been setting aside the maximum allowed for the last nine years—$9,500 a year, or a total of $85,000 in his case. His employer makes matching contributions (a formula that works out to $2,075 a year), the stock market has given him fabulous returns, and his money grows tax-deferred, which means he doesn't have to pay taxes until he withdraws funds for retirement, when he will likely be in a much lower tax bracket. In nine years, Sale's $85,000 has grown to $205,000.

With three more years to go until the oldest of his three sons starts college, he can borrow up to the maximum $50,000 from his pension. The 10 percent penalty for early withdrawals will not apply, as this counts as a loan to himself, not a withdrawal. His pension plan gives him five years to repay, with interest tied to the prime plus 1.5 percent—to himself. Sale will be losing the opportunity to earn what he could if he kept those retirement funds invested, but he will save the income taxes he would have paid on dividends and capital gains had he tried to save the same amount for college in a taxable account.

Parents can use regular IRAs for qualified education expenses (which include tuition, fees, books, supplies, and, for students attending at least half time, room and board) without incurring an additional 10 percent penalty, but they will have to pay income tax. However, the Taxpayers Relief

Act of 1997 (H.R. 2014) allows parents filing jointly with adjusted gross income (AGI) of under $150,000 (single filers must have AGI less than $95,000), beginning tax-year 1998, to put aside up to $500 a year for each child under age 18 in a special IRA-like fund. Unlike traditional IRAs, Education IRA contributions are not deductible, although qualified withdrawals are tax-free, as long as they're used for qualified higher education expenses (which include tuition, fees, books, supplies and equipment, and room and board for students who attend college at least half time).

Another new individual retirement arrangement, called the Roth IRA, allows taxpayers with AGI less than $95,000 if they're single and $150,000 if they're married and file jointly to set aside up to $2,000 a year. As with the Education IRA just mentioned, these contributions are not tax-deductible, and qualified withdrawals are tax-free (as long as the Roth IRA is at least five years old, and you are over age 59½). Before age 59½, you don't have to pay the 10 percent penalty, but do have to pay tax on the income portion of withdrawals that are used for education (or other qualified purposes). A spokesperson for Sen. William Roth explains, "Say you made $6,000 in contributions into a Roth IRA and over the years that money earned $4,000 income. If you take a distribution of $7,000, you'd pay tax only on $1,000 because the other $6,000 would be after-tax money."

Ask a financial adviser if rolling over your traditional IRA into a Roth IRA, or making future contributions into the newer vehicle makes economic sense for you. Or check out an on-line Roth IRA calculator such as www.datachimp.com/articles/rothira/rothiracalc.htm. (It is only beneficial to roll over an existing IRA into a Roth IRA if you can afford to pay tax on the rollover from non-IRA funds. If you pay for that tax with IRA money, you essentially wipe out future tax benefits of the Roth IRA.)

Take out a home-equity loan

Owning a home and building up equity in your home can be a great source of collateral you can use to help pay for college. There are many advantages to taking out a home-equity loan over other sources of borrowed funds. First, unlike interest on other loans, home-equity loan interest is tax deductible if you itemize deductions. Second, home-equity loans usually carry lower rates than other personal bank loans. Third, selective schools often factor in assets such as home equity (unlike most other schools and federal financial aid formulas) but do not count most forms of consumer debt—except first and second mortgages on your home. To the extent that you borrow against your home (or pay down other debts with home-equity loans), you reduce the amount of your assets in the eyes of financial aid officers, and, therefore, lower the amount you end up having to contribute to college.

Earn college credit

Academically gifted kids can take Advanced Placement (AP) courses in up to 16 subjects during high school. Passing scores on several AP exams can save you up to a year in college tuition (or approximately 15 college credits).

High schoolers can also earn college credit at more than 2,800 accredited institutions by scoring satisfactorily on any of 34 College Level Examination Program (CLEP) exams, at more than 1,300 CLEP test centers in the United States. Each exam costs $43, plus the test administration fee (generally $10). Each college has its own maximum on the number of CLEP credits it will grant. For more information, call CLEP at 609-771-7865 or check out its Web site (www.collegeboard.com/clep/html/indx001.html).

Start out at a community college

Many community colleges provide excellent, inexpensive two-year programs. Living home those two years can also save a bundle in room and board. After two years, students can transfer to a four-year institution. The degree will list the school from which the student graduates.

Tom Sale plans to encourage his three sons, ages 6, 12, and 14, to attend the local community college for the first two years. "Not only is our community college an excellent institution," he says, "but it guarantees that every course credit is completely transferable to any university or college in the country."

Student jobs

Many high schoolers have part-time jobs and can sock away most of their earnings while living at home. Just monitor your child's ability to juggle school, work, and social life (as we discussed in Chapter 1). You don't want slipping grades to rule out possible academic scholarships. Your child may consider taking a year off before college and work to save up as much as she can. Some jobs may even provide tuition assistance.

Armed Service

If your child is willing to commit to active duty after graduation with the Army, Navy, Air Force, or Marines, the Reserve Officer Training Corp. (ROTC) will pay a portion of college costs. High-school guidance counselors or local recruiters can provide more details.

Financial Aid

THERE IS, INDEED, a large pool of funds available for college students, some based on financial need, others on academic excellence, and some with neither type of requirement. In 1997–98, some $55 billion (compared with $28 billion a decade ago) was disbursed in the form of grants and loans, from federal, state, and institutional sources.

To find out what kind of financial aid your child may be eligible to receive, you first must fill out a form called the Free Application for Federal Student Aid (FAFSA). You can get one from high school guidance counselors, some public libraries, through the Internet (www.fafsa.ed.gov), or by calling 800-4-FED-AID (800-433-3243). Usually within four weeks after sending your completed application, FAFSA will send you a Student Aid Report that will summarize the information you provided and give you your expected family contribution (EFC)—the amount your family is expected to pay toward college expenses in the form of current income, savings, or loans. Federal as well as many private sources of financial aid base eligibility for aid on the EFC.

Parents who are secretive with their kids about their personal finances may find this process uncomfortable. It's tough to file the paperwork without your kids seeing your income and assets, as you and they must sign the FAFSA. Some parents refuse to divulge this information to their kids or to colleges. "These days when that happens, colleges say to parents, 'If you won't play your role, we won't play ours,'" says the College Board's James Montague. Unfortunately, that shuts out the kid, from both financial aid and from the opportunity to enter a new, more adult relationship with their parents.

When parents share such sensitive information with their kids, they demonstrate trust and give kids a more realistic picture of the family. Suddenly kids can either appreciate how hard their parents have worked and the success that created, or they can see in black and white (and maybe red) the limits of more modest family finances. Either way, opening the books can open constructive and candid discussions that are bound to help kids align their expectations to their given reality.

Montague encourages parents to complete the EFC a couple of years in advance of when their kids will apply to college. "Otherwise, students who are not aware of where their parents are financially may be encouraged to pursue all these wonderful colleges. At the last minute, some parents may pull the rug out and say they can't afford those. That's not fair. Students deserve to go into the process well aware of what the limitations are."

Parents who are divorced can probably avoid divulging their personal finances to their ex-spouse. The custodial parent—the one with whom the child lives most of the year—fills out the FAFSA. In most cases, colleges will also contact the noncustodial parent and ask him or her to fill out other forms to get some sense of their ability to contribute. "There's no hard and fast rule about whether they contact the noncustodial parent," says Montague. "The more expensive the college, the more likely they'll contact the other parent."

Parents should generally expect to foot about one-third of the tuition bill. The College Board Web site has a worksheet (www.collegeboard.com/html/calculator000.html) that helps you calculate the expected family contribution (EFC), how much you need to save to do so, and how repayment of student loans can impact your own and your children's future finances. The difference between the cost of one year's college and the EFC determines your financial need—the amount you will be eligible to obtain through the various forms of financial aid.

There are many ways to reduce the value of assets you need to report on the financial aid forms. Anna and Robert Leider, authors of *Don't Miss Out: The Ambitious Student's Guide to Financial Aid* (Dearborn Trade, 1995), suggest:

■ Business assets count less than personal assets—only 60 percent of a business's net worth, up to $80,000, is factored into the financial aid equation. So it makes sense to turn any sources of income from hobbies or property into a business if you can. You may even want to consider shifting assets into a sub-S corporation, with your family owning 51 percent, while non-immediate family members hold 49 percent. Transferring $50,000 of such assets this way will first reduce your net worth to $30,000, and then whittle that down to $15,300.

■ Use some of your savings to pay down your home mortgage, because the federal financial aid formulas ignore home equity. However, the institution's aid officer may expect families to borrow against cushy, mortgage-free homes before granting you financial aid.

■ Use OPM (other people's money). One possible source is your boss. Some employers will reimburse you for some tuition costs. Grandparents who want to help can make direct payments to the school without having that count toward their $10,000 gift tax limit.

Many financial aid consultants charge into the hundreds of dollars to help you fill out the forms and claim to help maximize your chances of getting financial aid. Be careful. There are plenty of scams out there (www.finaid.org lists several of them and offers tips for spotting scam artists and also lists several consultants, their fees, and services). Not only do you want to avoid the chance of getting duped, you also shouldn't rob your kids of the opportunity to hone their investigative and analytical skills. Point them in the direction of free help from their high school guidance counselor, local library, the financial aid office of the college your teen plans to attend, or on-line services such as FinAid or Fast WEB (www.fastweb.com). Then enjoy watching their faces light up with pride as they authoritatively share with you all the neat sources of financial aid and other data they unearth.

Nellie Mae, the largest nonprofit provider of student and parent education loans in the United States, provides detailed information about financial aid options in its free 30-page guide to planning for college called "Steps to Success" (call 800-367-8848). Other publishers of college aid information include Barron's, Peterson's, The College Board, and The Princeton Review. Your public library reference section is likely to have shelves and shelves of such guide books.

By many measures, competition is heating up for financial aid. About 76 percent of freshmen sought aid in 1996, compared with 66 percent 10 years ago. As well, the number of 18-year-olds is expected to grow from 3.7 million in 1997 to 4.1 million in 2006. When you factor in inflation, the value of many forms of aid has actually decreased or remained level.

What are your chances of getting financial aid? James Montague gives different messages about financial aid availability to different families, depending on which end of the economic spectrum they belong. "I reassure less-advantaged students and their families that there is money available. Instead of worrying about money, I warn them that they should make sure their kids take the right courses and do well in high school." Students who look like attractive candidates academically will get the first crack at available aid over students with equal need with lower grades. Students from higher income families will be eligible for some aid, but more of it will be in the form of loans, not grants.

Scholarships and Grants

Obviously, you would prefer your financial aid package to comprise mostly grants and scholarships, not loans. Some experts recommend avoiding early acceptance because the school will figure it doesn't have to lure an already committed student with a mouth-watering financial aid package. Even interviewing on campus may make a student seem over-eager, and may result in more loans than grants.

Like financial aid consultants, scholarship search services will offer to take your money to help you find sources of "free money." FinAid's Web page also lists dozens of services and their fees. FinAid warns that several such services use the same databases, so searches through each service will yield the same findings, even though costs can vary widely. For instance, Epperson Analysis and Advisery charges $39, while JVL College Aid Service charges $159—

yet both use the same College Academic Service (CAS) database of 300,000 sources of nonfederal financial aid. If you are going to use a commercial service, FinAid's charts can help you find one of the cheapest ones for each database.

Once again, if you nudge your kids to do a little homework, they are bound to find plenty of free ways to search for scholarships. High school guidance officers can tell them about scholarships offered through the school. Some high schools and public libraries have software programs that list grants and scholarships. Local Rotary clubs and similar local groups in your area may provide scholarships. Gently remind your kids that the colleges to which they have applied may have their own scholarship and grant programs, based not just on financial need, but also athletic or academic performance.

If your family is wired, your kids can find plenty of scholarship resources. See the Appendix for descriptions of the following and other sites.

■ FastWEB (www.fastweb.com) lets high schoolers create a student profile and will search its list of 275,000 private-sector scholarships, fellowships, grants, and loans for those the student may be eligible to receive. Students can also create a mailbox to which FastWEB will forward information about new sources of money that match the student's profile.

■ Scholarship Resource Network (www.rams.com/srn/execsrch.htm), the College Board's ExPAN Scholarship Search (www.collegeboard.org/fundfinder/bin.fundfind01.pl), CollegeNET MACH 25 (www.collegenet.com/mach25), and SallieMae's Online Scholarship Service (scholarships.salliemae.com) contain searchable scholarship databases.

■ In addition, www.studentcontests.com lists several hundred contests, some of which give cash prizes or full scholarships. The site belongs to Scott Pendelton, author of *The Ultimate Guide to Student Contests, Grades 7–12* (Walker & Company, 1997).

Federal Pell Grants

Pell Grants are typically awarded to families whose expected family contribution (EFC) is below a ceiling determined each year. These grants, which do not need to be repaid, provide up to $2,700 a year to the neediest U.S. students, which covers about one-third the average cost of a four-year public school today. At its peak in the 1970s, the maximum Pell Grant paid for three-quarters of the cost. That's because the average Pell Grant was worth $50 less in 1992 than in 1982 after inflation, while during roughly the same period, college costs rose more than 200 percent at private schools and 153 percent at public institutions.

Federal Supplemental Educational Opportunity Grant

The FSEOG is for students with exceptional financial need. The maximum annual FSEOG was $4,000 for the 1997–98 school year, which families also do not need to pay back.

Federal Work Study

FWS helps students with financial need to earn money to help pay education expenses. The program, run through the school, arranges on- or off-campus jobs for undergrads that pay at least minimum wage (more for students who can perform more highly skilled jobs), typically for 10 to 15 hours a week. The program attempts to place students in community service jobs or work related to the student's area of study. The amount that work-study students can earn cannot exceed the FWS award, which is based on when they apply, their degree of need, and the funding level of the school.

Federal Perkins Loans

Undergrads can borrow up to $3,000 a year (in 1998–99) in Perkins Loans, which carry the lowest interest rate of all education loans (5 percent in 1998–99). Students have up to

10 years to repay the loan, beginning nine months after they leave college.

Federal Stafford Loans

Private lending institutions write these loans up to $2,625 to freshmen, $3,500 to sophomores, and $5,500 per year for juniors and seniors attending school at least half time. The below-market interest rate on Federal Stafford Loans is variable, but as of this writing cannot exceed 8.25 percent. The "grace period" before repayment begins is six months after college.

There are two types of Stafford Loans: subsidized and unsubsidized. Students with the greatest financial need (determined by the FAFSA) can get subsidized Stafford Loans for which the government pays the interest while the student is in school, during the grace period, and during any authorized deferment periods. Eligibility for an unsubsidized Federal Stafford Loan is not need-based. Students must pay interest on the loan while in school, during the grace period, and during any authorized deferment periods, although recipients can postpone interest payments while in-school and during the grace period by "capitalizing" the interest (adding it on to the principal amount).

Even if you can afford to foot a large portion of tuition, it might be wise for your child to take out one of these federal loans. Unlike private funding sources, repayment doesn't begin until after your child leaves school. Meantime, you can keep your money invested in higher interest-bearing investments and help your child pay off the loan later. Parents can't assume the promissory note. They can make or help with payments, but less than 10 percent of parents do.

Federal PLUS Loans

Parents can also borrow federal funds for their children's education (enrolled at least half time). Parents with good credit can borrow enough to cover the total per-year cost of education, minus any financial aid received. The borrowed PLUS money goes directly to the school, and parents have 10 years to repay the loans, beginning 60 days after the funds are disbursed. The variable interest rate has a cap of 9 percent.

Private Financial Aid

Education loans are also available through banks or student loan organizations, such as Nellie Mae's EXCEL loans. Since 1992, federal student and parent loans have been available for families at any income level. Some parents feel guilty if they make their child borrow to pay for college. Diane Saunders, Nellie Mae's vice president of public affairs, counsels parents not to feel they need to shoulder the entire burden themselves. She says that because the student is the primary beneficiary of the education, they should take a stake in paying for it. Parents should make sure their children understand the responsibility they are assuming when they take out a loan.

Many families cobble together funds from a variety of sources—grants, scholarships, loans, and work-study programs. *Table 5.5* on page 168 shows how Ed, a college freshman from New York, covered his $31,520-a-year annual tuition and expenses at the University of Pennsylvania. The package included $3,800 from his parents' expected contribution, $2,960 from his own expected contribution, a $8,510 scholarship from the school, a $1,450 Pell Grant, $4,000 from a Federal Supplemental Educational Opportunity Grant (FSEOG), $2,175 from work study (including earnings from jobs during semester and summer), a $3,000 Perkins Loan, $3,000 in a Penn Guaranteed Loan, and a $2,625 Stafford Loan.

As a former Eagle Scout, Ed would have been eligible for a Boy Scout scholarship too, but that wouldn't have lowered his loans or his parents' contribution. Instead, the university would have lowered its scholarship by that amount.

Repaying Loans

NOT ONLY ARE MORE STUDENTS borrowing for college, but they are also borrowing more. In the mid-1980s, Nellie Mae says, financial aid associations considered graduates to have a financial burden if their debt-to-income ratio (that's monthly student loan debt to monthly take-home pay) was 8 percent or more. Today students are graduating with an average ratio of 10 percent—half have less than 8 percent, and half have more.

The average private-college student these days is borrowing about $17,600 over four years, and a public-school student's four-year total is $13,000. Graduates don't always find cushy salaries to help them make those monthly school-loan payments. Graduate student loans average $24,500 and professional students (medical, law, and dental) average $48,500. In the previous generation or two, unless students got into medical or law school, they managed to get through college without huge loans looming over them. When aspiring doctors and lawyers graduated, they could feel comfort knowing their expected future income would enable them to repay their school loans. That's not always so today. Anne Stockwell points out in her book, *The Guerrilla Guide to Mastering Student Loan Debt* (Harper Perennial, 1997), that over the last 13 years medical students' first-year income has increased by 68 percent, but their debt on graduation has increased 248 percent.

"My son will come out of college with $40,000 in loans," says Barbara Perman, owner of Moving On, a business in Amherst, Massachusetts, that provides consulting and management services to people moving. "I felt he had to be involved in the decision. So I brought him with me to talk to my financial counselor. We looked at the statistics of likely income that students earn after graduating from different schools. He could have gone to other schools and incurred less debt, but he chose the more expensive option.

He knows he has 10 years to pay it off. We discussed the concrete compromises he might have to make to afford his payments, such as living at home and driving a second-hand car. At least he has some idea about what he's getting himself into."

Will your child be able to pay off his or her college loans? Most of the nearly 8 million student borrowers, who owe about $30 billion in student loans, can and do repay their debt. In fact, the student-loan default rate decreased in fiscal year 1995 (the most recent reported figures as of this writing) to 10.4 percent from 10.7 percent the previous year, and 22.4 percent at its height in 1990.

Lower interest rates undoubtedly helped improve repayments. But lower default rates do not mean students are finding it easier to repay their loans. In fact, the Department of Education says it deserves most of the credit, pointing to its increased collection and accountability efforts. The government has gotten tougher—it now devotes more resources to collection and no longer allows student loans to be discharged as a result of bankruptcy. It has also gotten smarter—is has beefed up entrance and exit counseling, and offers a wider range of repayment options.

Despite the overall improvement, "One scary trend is that the default rate for private four-year students, which has generally been pretty low, increased for the first time ever, to 6.9 percent in fiscal 1995 from 6.3 percent in fiscal 1994," points out Diane Saunders of Nellie Mae. "Generally they are considered the cream of the crop and get the best rates. Students are borrowing at much higher levels and their earnings are not offsetting that."

Parents can play an important role in outlining the responsibilities of assuming such substantial debt, and the consequences of not paying it back. Many schools are pitching in by helping kids who take out loans better understand the numbers. Nellie Mae's Debt Management EDvisor is an interactive program to help students understand the impact of financing an education through borrowing. Its worksheets and calculators determine budgets, estimate loan payments, and record and update loan portfolios. You can access this and more at its Web site (www.nelliemae.org)—but the EDvisor part only runs on a Windows (PC) operating system.

You can explain to your kids that they must start repaying their loans six months after they graduate or leave school. Many lenders, such as Nellie Mae, offer student borrowers opportunities to save hundreds, and sometimes thousands, of dollars on loan repayments. For instance, students with a perfect repayment record who have taken out the most common type of student loan, the Stafford Loan, through Nellie Mae's Student Loan EDvantages program, either get a 2 percent interest-rate reduction or don't have to make the last six months of their repayments. As well, borrowers who sign up for automatic deductions from their savings or checking accounts for loan payments can clip another quarter of a percent off their interest rate. Graduates who are unemployed or otherwise financially unable to repay their obligation have many repayment and deferment options available (see *Table 5.4*, page 166).

The problem is, many students have no idea whether or not they are headed for trouble. Saunders recalls asking a college intern about the balance of her student loan. "She told me she didn't know and was scared to find out. She figured she would deal with it after she graduated." Unfortunately, by then her choices will be more limited. "Many students are virgin credit consumers," says Saunders. "They are borrowing more at earlier periods before they're on their own and have to manage repayments and living expenses together. If they're not paying anything back yet, it's easier to sign on the dotted line without thinking about how much they're borrowing. They don't understand until they sign that first school-loan repayment check."

By that time, they may be up to their ears in credit-card debt as well as student loans. Nellie Mae says 65 percent of its undergraduate borrowers have credit cards with an average balance of $2,226 and an average credit limit of $6,122. Graduate students with Nellie Mae loans have an average of seven credit cards and an average balance of $5,800, with an average available credit limit of $15,000!

Nellie Mae's Web site (www.nelliemae.org) has extensive information on repayment options if your graduate gets into trouble. The bottom of its home page has an interactive debt-counseling tool with calculators and worksheets to help graduates and undergraduates punch in what they expect to earn (see *Table 5.3* on the following page), their expenses, and their outstanding loans. It indicates if they are likely to come out in the black or in the red, and walks them through the kinds of decisions they'll have to make about adjusting expenses. Saunders recommends that current students run through the exercise to figure out what level of borrowing they can handle now in order to keep themselves out of trouble after they graduate.

The College Board's Web site (www.collegeboard. com/html/calculator000.html) includes a list of estimated starting incomes for college graduates in various fields, which students will need to use in Nellie Mae's debt-counseling worksheets.

One school in the forefront of encouraging students to manage their debt is Brigham Young University, which uses a combination of workbooks, videos, and its Web site (ar.byu.edu/financialpath) to expose students to exercises that include estimating education costs, financial resources, financial aid, expected future income, and borrowing costs.

Deferments and Forbearances

Students who have trouble repaying subsidized Stafford Loans can ask for a deferment under certain circumstances, such as if they are unemployed or go back to school. With a deferment, the interest rate clock stops and the federal government picks up the interest payments during the defer-

TABLE 5.3

Estimated Starting Incomes of College Graduates

Major Field of Study	Estimated Starting Income
Accounting	$27,787
Advertising	21,627
Agriculture	24,134
Chemical Engineering	40,341
Chemistry	28,386
Civil Engineering	29,547
Communications	21,640
Computer Science	32,446
Education	22,685
Electrical Engineering	34,979
Financial Administration	26,630
General Business Administration	23,760
Geology	28,414
Hotel, Restaurant, Inst. Management	23,713
Human Ecology/ Home Economics	21,053
Industrial Engineering	33,348
Journalism	20,587
Liberal Arts/Arts and Letters	20,860
Marketing, Sales	24,607
Mathematics	26,415
Mechanical Engineering	35,369
Natural Resources	22,554
Nursing	29,868
Personnel Administration	22,923
Physics	27,087
Retailing	22,002
Social Science	22,333
Telecommunications	20,680

Source: The College Board

ment period. Students with unsubsidized Stafford Loans can ask for a forbearance, which allows them to take a breather from monthly payments, but interest continues to accrue and is added to the outstanding loan balance.

Graduated Repayment Plans

Such plans allow students to start out making lower monthly payments, which gradually increase over time as income is likely to rise. The loan still matures in 10 years.

Loan Consolidation

Students with very high debt from numerous lenders can lower their monthly payments and extend the life of the loan for up to 30 years by folding all the loans into one. Saunders cautions, "Don't use this just to have one payment; it's an extremely expensive convenience. Use it only if you can't handle your monthly payments."

Income-Sensitive Repayment

This gives students a chance to work with the lender to repay according to their income. Payments are stretched out for up to 15 years, which increases the cost of the loan. *Table 5.4* on the following page compares the ultimate cost of a $15,000 loan under each repayment option.

Saunders cautions students to "try to hang in there with a standard 10-year payment if you can. Make other sacrifices before negotiating an alternative repayment plan, because the standard payments will only get easier as long as your salary increases." However, if a graduate does run into problems, the most important thing is not to try to avoid the situation. The minute a student is concerned about defaulting on a student loan he should contact the lender. Most lenders are willing to work out a more manageable repayment plan.

TABLE 5.4

Repayment Options for Federal Family Education Loans

(numbers rounded)

	Standard Repayment	Graduated Repayment	Loan-Consolidation Repayment	Income-Sensitive Repayment
Amount borrowed	$15,000	$15,000	$15,000	$15,000
Interest rate	8 percent	8 percent	8 percent	8 percent
Initial payment (monthly)	$182	$126[1]	$144	$100[2]
Length of loan repayment	10 years	10 years	15 years	15 years
Total interest paid (over life of loan)	$6,839	$7,906	$10,802	$14,740
Total paid (over life of loan)	$21,839	$22,906	$25,802	$29,740

[1] Graduated repayment starts out with smaller monthly payments which gradually increase over a five-year period (to $177 at end of 48 months) and then, in this example, become fixed after the fifth year (at the 60th month) at $230.

[2] Income-sensitive example is based on an initial student-loan debt-to-income ratio of 4 percent at an initial income of $30,000 a year. With this option, the minimum payment is $100, and the borrower must at least pay interest only; no payment can be more than three times any other payment. The loan payment would eventually increase to $143 a month at the midpoint of repayment, and to $236 a month for the last three years of repayment.

Source: Nellie Mae

Shopping for the Right College

OBVIOUSLY MONEY is a key factor when shopping for college. But don't rule out a school your child likes just because its cost is beyond your financial means. Colleges that charge higher tuition tend to have more funds available for financial aid.

Conversely, don't assume the college with the highest price tag is the best for your child. Also consider location, size, academic programs and reputation, and extracurricular activities. The most important factor to consider, says Nellie Mae, is which college your child most wants to attend.

"We agreed to pay complete tuition, books, and everything at a private college, as long as our daughter, Sarah, picked a school we felt was worth the extra money," says Donna Levine of New Haven, Connecticut. But Donna didn't feel her daughter's initial choice was worth the high cost. "She started talking about Syracuse University (a private school in upstate New York with 14,500 students), and we said we're not going to pay $30,000 a year for a large school when she could find a large state school that would be much cheaper." Sarah ultimately chose Barnard (a private school in Manhattan affiliated with Ivy League Columbia University that costs about the same as Syracuse but has 2,300 all-female students).

Computer software by The College Board and Peterson's, available at many public libraries and high school guidance offices, can help you search according to many categories such as location, size, and cost. CollegeView's FullView Edition even gives a multimedia "tour" through several campuses.

Although the University of Pennsylvania was the most expensive choice among the four schools Ed was considering (see *Table 5.5* on the following page), and the financial aid package was mostly in the form of loans, that is the school he ultimately chose.

Ed fell in love with the University of Pennsylvania when he visited for a weekend. He felt he would have the social and religious element that would make him feel connected. His mother and grandfather went there, so there was also an emotional connection for him. Because he doesn't know what area he wants to major in, Ed wants a big school with a number of departments that are excellent. Last, it was

TABLE 5.5

Comparison of College Financial Packages

	A joint Columbia University/ Jewish Theological Seminary, New York, NY	State University of New York (SUNY) at Binghamton, Binghamton, NY	Brandeis University, Waltham, MA	University of Pennsylvania, Philadelphia, PA
Costs	$28,080	$11,115	$30,985	$31,520
Grants/ scholarships	$20,068	$4,302	$19,460	$9,960
Parent contribution	$1,387	0	$3,000	$3,800
Student contribution	$3,000	0	$3,000	$2,960
Work study	$1,000	0	$1,500	$2,175
Loans	$2,625	$6,813	$4,025	$12,625
School size	170	9,349	2,950	19,000

not too close to home. "I didn't want to be able to go home to do my laundry," he says, "but I wanted to be close enough to visit my family without having to hop on a plane." Ed's mother encouraged him to follow his heart, as long as he had his eyes open to the financial consequences. She also assured him that she intended to help him repay a portion of his student loan.

Living Away from Home

HOWEVER MUCH OR LITTLE responsibility you have given your kids so far, before they trot off to college, you and your child should sketch out a budget. Kathleen M. Payea, associate director of financial aid services at New York City–based College Scholarship Service (CSS) (a division of the College Board), estimates that a student on a tight budget can live on $6,504 during a nine-month academic year, or $9,686 on a moderate budget. Of course, cost of living will differ from region to region, and will be higher in a city than in a rural area.

M. Melinda Tschappat, former banker and coauthor of *The Pitfalls of Plastic Credit Cards,* suggests the following breakdown of living expenses to keep spending in line with gross (before taxes) income:

20–23 percent	housing and utilities
17–19	taxes
8–9	debt payments
8–9	food
8–9	savings
7–9	entertainment, hobbies
7–9	vacations
7–8	transportation
4–5	insurance
4	clothing and personal care
3–4	gifts and contributions
1–2	medical

The national average as of 1997 for room and board at a private college is $4,954, or $3,929 for a public school, according to the *Money College Guide '98.* One way to save on the housing and possibly food for students living on campus is for your coed to apply for a position in their dorm as a resident assistant (RA).

All the advice in the previous chapters has been geared to help you prepare your kids for what will be the first taste of independence for many students. Moving away from home can be a rude awakening for kids who have limited experience doing their own laundry, shopping for food or personal sundries, and managing a budget. Obviously, the more responsibility you give them before you launch them into the ivory-tower world, the easier they will find the transition.

TABLE 5.6

Tips for Getting to and through College

1. It's never too late to start saving for college.

2. It's never too early to start saving for college.

3. When calculating what you need to save for college, expect to cover about one-third of projected college costs.

4. Don't be discouraged if you can't save that much! Save whatever you can, as early and as regularly as you can.

5. When you finish paying for things—such as diapers, day care, or a new car—keep that amount in your budget, but divert the money to college savings.

6. For kids 13 and younger, stick to the stock market—but diversify.

7. Keep savings in the parents' names—at least starting the year before your kids apply for college.

8. Take advantage of the new Education IRA's tax-free accounts.

9. Consider funding up to $50,000 in college costs by borrowing from your 401(k) pension or by taking out a home-equity loan.

10. To cut back on costs, have academically gifted kids earn college credit through Advanced Placement or CLEP exams.

11. Don't ignore community colleges for the first two years. They are much less expensive than public or private four-year schools, and many credits are transferable to most other institutions.

12. Regardless of your family's financial standing, investigate free money from scholarships and grants (the high school guidance counselor, public library, and Internet can identify money your child might be eligible to receive).

13. You don't need to be poor to apply for financial aid.

14. Don't feel guilty expecting your child to take some stake in their education, with a student loan.

15. Make sure your child understands the terms of their student loans: what their monthly payments will be after graduation, and the likely income from different career options in their field.

16. Don't assume the most expensive college is the best place for your child.

17. Don't make financial factors the only criteria for choosing a college.

Chapter 6

Helping Your Child

Nab the Right

First Job

HELPING YOUR KIDS LAND A GREAT JOB IS LIKELY to have a profound effect on their financial well being. A career makes the single biggest economic impact on a person's life. People read investment self-help books and spend thousands of dollars hiring financial consultants to help them eke out a point or two higher return on their savings, which represent, on average, 4 percent of after-tax earnings. But what we earn from work has a far greater impact on future wealth than what we earn from our investments.

Of course you want your kids to find meaningful, fulfilling work, not just the biggest paycheck. Marsha Sinetar, author of *Do What You Love, The Money Will Follow* (Paulist Press/Dell, 1989, $11.95), says you can have a great job and the big bucks. But not all kids know what they want or what they love. Many young adults who have identified a career path may not have the skills, contacts, or road map to navigate their way to that path. Parents can play an important role in helping them get the job of their dreams.

As of mid-1998, unemployment, at 4.5 percent, was at a 24-year low and skilled, dynamic entry-level employees were in hot demand. The National Association of Colleges and Employers' 1998 Job Outlook Survey notes that nearly 70 percent of employer-respondents plan to hire more new graduates in 1998 than they did the year before—by 19.1 percent, in part because they cannot find enough experienced workers.

History shows that demographic and economic cycles can radically affect the job market, so even a slight recession could put a crimp in hiring. But even in these rosy conditions, not all young adults are landing fast-track, high-paying jobs. The Bureau of Labor Statistics says that 25 percent of college grads take jobs that don't require a bachelor's degree (by 2005 that figure is expected to reach 30 percent). Increasingly, employers are raising their standards, recruiting college graduates for jobs that in the past were filled by high school grads. Many new grads end up taking low-paying, low-benefit, low-prestige, no-future jobs like waiting tables, pumping gas, or checking out groceries—either because they have been unable to define what they want to do or because they don't know how to find better jobs. Employers only want candidates that meet high standards. Kids need all the help they can get, and you are in a unique position to guide them.

Understanding Your Role

BUT MANY PARENTS don't have a clue how to help. This chapter will show parents how to offer the most constructive and effective guidance to job-hunting kids. Some adults think they have all the answers from years of experience in the work world, and try to control their kids' job hunt. This chapter will help such parents identify a comfortable and meaningful role—without stepping on their kids' toes. You will learn how to guide them to identify goals, understand the job market, create a dynamic résumé, handle job interviews with panache, get through employment tests, target a job search, and evaluate offers.

Nella Barkley, cofounder of New York City–based career-counseling firm Crystal-Barkley, suggests that parents assume the role of coach and view their child as a "client" they are trying to help. "Don't cross the line of imposing yourself when you're unwanted," she warns. Playing coach stacks the odds in your favor that they will even listen to any advice you proffer. It's helpful to move as far from your parenting role as possible. Assuming a more professional relationship creates a sense of mutual respect that makes it possible for the young adult child to take advantage of the parents' skills, knowledge, and sophistication. "Parents have to accept responsibility for taking that tone," insists Barkley, author of *How to Help Your Child Land the Right Job (Without Being a Pain in the Neck)* (Workman Publishing, 1993). "It means really stepping back. If your 20-year-old is about to make a mistake, you can wisely say, 'Take another look at the match between your skills and the job,' instead of 'Can't you see that's not right for you; you were never good at that kind of thing.' Never ever say 'You ought to do this or that.'"

The main role of a parent/coach includes:

- Role-playing interview scenarios
- Allaying fear and anxiety
- Debriefing after meetings
- Helping to plan information gathering and interviews
- Evaluating progress

A coaching versus a parenting role can also prevent you from relying too much on your own preconceived notions about the workplace, which has changed profoundly since you pounded the pavement for your first entry-level job.

"If you haven't been in the job-seeking world in the last three years, you don't know what jobs are out there," insists Carol Rivchun, founder of Me Incorporated, a Cleveland Heights, Ohio, marketing consultancy. For example, Rivchun, former vice president of marketing and communications for the Greater Cleveland Growth Association, explains: "Five years ago when I was looking for a writer, I just needed a person who wrote. Two years ago when I was looking for a writer, I wouldn't have hired the world's best writer unless that person could also do desktop publishing." In the near future, when Rivchun hopes to create a Web site for her business, she will likely require that person to have on-line expertise as well.

It pays to get your kids thinking and preparing early about possible career paths. Waiting until after graduation from college to ponder what to do next means that your son or daughter will miss opportunities to explore potential careers and to gain experience before graduation that can give them an edge in getting meaningful and promising employment. Those who start early also have a better chance of finding out about different career options and ruling out those that end up not feeling right—while there is still time to switch academic majors and explore other directions.

Start as early as the end of freshman year, recommends Tina Acker, associate director of the University of Massachusetts Career Center. "Getting experience before graduation is an absolute must," she insists. "It will make all the difference in getting a job more quickly and at a higher level after graduation." By sophomore year, she says, students should begin to explore work co-op jobs, internships, and volunteer programs that can not only provide practical experience, but can also help students learn early if a career they had in mind is what they really want to pursue.

How should your child begin to hunt for a first job?

Her first step should be to look inside herself, not "out there" at the job market. Many experts concur that trying to second-guess what potential employers are looking for and then figuring out how to mold herself to one of those job descriptions is unlikely to generate exciting opportunities. First your child must decide what she wants and then she can figure out how to go after it. A wise approach is:

■ Ready—have the student take an internal inventory of his passions, values, and dreams.

■ Aim—identify and research industries, companies, and positions that may be a good match.

■ Fire—customize résumés; prepare for information meetings and interviews at those companies; and pursue the many job-search methods, from classified ads, networking, college career centers, and on-line career sites, to employment agencies and temp services.

Ready: Identifying Career Goals

PEOPLE THINK THE HIGHER they set their sights, the farther and more conspicuously they might fall. I couldn't disagree more. I believe there's more downside risk and less to gain by going for a mediocre, typical job than trying for the pot of gold. You don't have much to show for going the easy route, and it can be a blow to your ego if you're rejected. When you reach for the stars, not only is there more upside potential when you make it, there's also less potential humiliation if you fail (because who could reasonably expect you to succeed?).

By all means, encourage your kids not to get too practical, agrees Nella Barkley. Even in a tight job market, she insists that it is realistic to shoot for your dreams. "Jobs are created in fields that are shrinking, by people clever enough to see new needs in them," says Barkley. Job seekers "need to decide what their interests, aptitudes, and favorite skills are, and then bring them together and think about what they want to do—not what is possible to do or what they think they should do."

Employers pick up on and value a person's energy and enthusiasm. "Other skills can be acquired, but candidates who are responding to their internal mission will find a way to achieve their dreams," Barkley says. "Nothing is more practical."

Some kids have very idealistic career dreams. If your child wants to play for the NBA, become a rock star, or be the next Bill Gates, you'd be remiss in not pointing out the minuscule chances of attaining those precise goals. But you'd also be doing a disservice by trying to dissuade him or her from building a career, in some way, on those passions. Passion and attitude are key determinants of success.

"Kids are often urged to study subjects or chase activities that will look good on the résumé," notes Barkley. That's important, but don't pressure them into such pursuits at the expense of undertakings they love. "It's very damaging because in the end, it's the person, not the piece of paper, that gets the job."

"Dream with teenagers," urges Susan Quattrociocchi, Ph.D, director of the Northeast Tech Prep Consortium in Bellevue, Washington. "Get excited together about the vast possibilities in their future. But be realistic, too. Guide them gently by encouraging careers that closely match their natural abilities, and where you seriously think they will be happy. These may not necessarily be careers you would choose for yourself," she adds.

Nella Barkley suggests that instead of focusing on finding something to *be*, such as doctor or accountant, we should concentrate on naming significant goals. When a lawyer sees himself not just as a lawyer, but as someone who defends people's rights or preserves law and order, he's better equipped to triumph over the daily grind. The same technique works in job hunting.

Quattrociocchi calls a goal a dream with a deadline.

One way to turn dreams into goals is to create what she calls a job circle—actually, a series of concentric circles—that puts the job seeker's key interest in the middle. Around it she draws a larger circle, in which she lists all kinds of occupations related to that interest, or types of people she would enjoy working with. The outer circle lists types of organizations that pay people to perform the activities in the middle circle. *Illustration 6.1* shows what a job circle might look like for someone interested in computers. Help your kids brainstorm filling in the circles based on their own key interests.

Barkley points out that an American history major might certainly teach, but also may write novels set in 18th century America; put together tours to historical sites; become an archaeologist, anthropologist, art collector, cura-

ILLUSTRATION 6.1

Job Circle

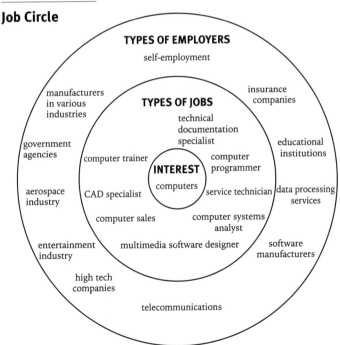

Source: Smart Choices! About Teen Jobs, by **Susan Quattrociocchi, Ph.D. (Steve Laing Communications, 1995)**

tor, or trader in rare books; research and reproduce furnishings; or restore historical buildings. If your daughter has always been drawn to music, careers in that field might include directing, producing, editing, and publicity. Basketball aficionados can consider opportunities in sports management, publicity, assistant coaching, sports writing, photography, or refereeing.

As parents, you can help your kids get a real-world idea of what jobs they are dreaming about entail. "Everything always sounds so glamorous," says Rivchun. "Kids all want to make movies. But they may not understand that videographers have to spend about 100 days writing scripts and rewriting and rewriting and going over details with people. They spend another 200 days looking for money, and maybe 20 days a year actually shooting a movie. So people who really like looking for money and not knowing what they're going to do this day next year and not knowing if they'll get a paycheck, if they still feel like they want to make movies, great. But it's never explained like that."

Rivchun originally planned to be a music teacher, but until her senior year of college, she'd never been in a classroom teaching. "If someone had encouraged me to talk to some teachers, it would have given me a better idea of what I was getting into," she says.

College career centers can be a great resource. For instance, at the University of Massachusetts, students can get real-world experience by applying for internships or work-study cooperative programs. UMass's University Computerized Alumni Network (UCAN) matches students with alumni mentors who can provide inside-track information and advice as well as pass along job leads that may not be advertised. The UMass Alumni Shadow Program matches students with alumni working in different fields to spend 36 hours on and off the job together. One student who shadowed an account director at an advertising agency notes,

TABLE 6.1

Top 10 Jobs for People Who . . .

LIKE TO KEEP LEARNING

software developer, physicist, diplomat, journalist, architect, benefits administrator, physician, teacher, writer, computer programmer

NEED TO PAY OFF STUDENT LOANS RIGHT AWAY

investment banker, financial analyst, management consultant, construction manager, banker, service sales representative (potentially), stockbroker, court reporter, carpenter, marketing executive

CAN'T STAND TIES OR PANTYHOSE

computer programmer, artist, writer, actor, petroleum engineer, coach, philosopher, zoologist, anthropologist, child-care worker

HAVE "TYPE-A" PERSONALITIES

attorney, investment banker, management consultant, pilot, military officer, baseball player, coach, astronaut, stockbroker, architect

LONG FOR UNPREDICTABLE DAYS

detective/private investigator, FBI agent, police officer, restaurateur, firefighter, musician, advertising executive, petroleum engineer, promoter, agent

LOVE PEOPLE

teacher, human resources manager, guidance counselor, career counselor, psychologist, social worker, child-care worker, physical therapist, fund-raiser, hotel manager

LIKE TO WORK WITH THEIR HANDS

carpenter, mechanic, dentist, machinist, zoologist, printer, robotics engineer, avionics technician, physician, chef

Source: Guide to Your Career, by Alan B. Bernstein, C.S.W., P.C. and Nicholas R. Schaffrin (Princeton Review, 1998)

"My day was spent looking at all the different departments involved in advertising. I am still unclear if this is the road I want to take. I do know that this program taught me more in one day than I have learned in any classroom."

One way to enhance marketable skills, especially during a period of unemployment or underemployment, is to sign up for classes listed in *Table 6.2, below.*

TABLE 6.2

Classes Worth Their Weight in Gold

- Business Writing
- Grant Writing
- Promotions/Public Relations
- Speech/Business Presentations
- Sales/Selling Principles
- Time Management
- Human Relations/Interpersonal Communications
- Marketing
- Language

Reprinted with permission from *Major in Success*, by Patrick Combs, Ten Speed Press, Berkeley, California.

Aim: Understanding the Job Market

TODAY'S WORKPLACE IS more fractured than it was when you were starting out. Companies are besieged by sudden spurts of downsizing and reengineering; they are flatter, with fewer layers of management; and they are more high-tech and entrepreneurial. Although the media play up that we are becoming more and more of a service economy, don't ignore manufacturing companies, which anticipate hiring 36 percent more college grads in 1998 than the previous year, compared with service companies, which plan a 16.1

percent increase in college hiring, according to the National Association of Colleges and Employers' 1998 Job Outlook Survey.

Meanwhile, the workforce is better educated, with cross training in multiple skills and experience. Generation Xers are generally more interested in flexibility with job sharing, non–nine-to-five work schedules, and telecommuting; more likely to change jobs every several years; and more likely to switch careers at least once during their work life.

"Whether by choice or necessity," says Quattrociocchi, "people are now creating their own work, either by creating their own business or by piecing together several jobs." She calls them "new century jobs" and notes that in 1995, two-thirds of American workers held traditional jobs while the other third, almost 39 million workers, had new century jobs. By 2010, half of Americans will be new century workers. New century work is characterized by:

■ Fewer permanent full-time positions, but a new business is born in the United States every eight seconds

■ 40-hour work week jobs are being replaced by temporary, contract, or consultant positions

■ Higher demand for specialists with good technical skills than for generalists

■ Companies that have downsized are combining tasks so that one person can do the work of several

If nothing else, it's an interesting time to launch a career. It's also a time to evaluate what skills employers demand. According to *Investing for Life: A Simplified Guide to the Complex World of Investments and Personal Finance for Teenagers* (Investment Education Institute and the National Association of Investors Corporation, 1997), employers are looking for candidates who not only have education and experience in their field, but also can demonstrate:

■ Work ethic—prompt, neat, has a positive attitude

■ Basic skills—reading, writing, math, and reasoning

■ Computer literacy—can use computers on the job

- Dependability—able to follow instructions
- Teamwork—works well with others
- Communication—can share information and ideas
- Responsibility—works well without supervision
- Initiative—applies knowledge in new situations
- Openness—eager to grow and learn on the job

You and your kids may have noticed that only two job requirements above—basic skills and computer literacy—have anything to do with education or experience; the rest relate to attitude. Without basic skills, most doors will remain locked. But given two equally skilled candidates, the one more likely to get through a given door will also demonstrate they possess the softer traits: ability to get along with and work with others, motivation, and even passion.

These are not qualities kids can acquire in college classrooms. If they don't have them by now, it's doubtful that you can instill these characteristics in your kids. But you can drive home the point that motivation, passion, and a serious work ethic are likely to affect their chance of success in any field.

The problem many parents fear most is that their kid isn't motivated to launch a career. How do you glue financial wings on your young slacker who has only vague, if any, plans beyond the college graduation party? You may not be able to inject ambition into your kid's veins, but at least you can avoid supporting his doing nothing.

As a newly minted journalism grad, I presented this very issue to my initially patient parents. I was languishing at home after graduation, partying till the wee hours with friends, sleeping late, and showing no sign of direction or intention to find a job. After two weeks, my parents handed me the Sunday classified section, gave me train and lunch money to go from our New York suburban home to Manhattan, and—they dispute this, but I clearly recall—told me not to come home until I found a job. I answered several ads, mostly from employment agencies. By the end of the day, I had accepted my only offer: to be secretary to the vice president of media relations in a financial public-relations firm, with the promise that I would have opportunities to write, learn, and move up.

The tactic may or may not work with your kid, but by refusing to support the kind of confusion and terror that initially paralyzed me, my parents prodded me to take action. When you don't know where you want to go, almost anyplace can be a starting point.

Today there are countless places to start a job search. Your child's college career center may have computer programs that list occupations and their wages, employment outlook, aptitudes, and work settings. Such programs can also list occupations you may want to consider based on your interests, abilities, and work preferences (based on an assessment test included in the program). Other programs let you search a database of potential employers around the country, in an array of industries.

Barkley recommends that before job seekers start pounding the pavement, they should survey the employment landscape. Encourage them to learn what different jobs in different industries and companies might be like, and to identify problems and needs in those industries and companies that the job seeker might be able to help fix.

Job seekers can identify industries and companies in them by calling the local chamber of commerce or nearest chapter of related professional trade associations, and by surfing the growing list of on-line career sites (The Riley Guide at www.dbm.com lists, describes, and offers links to more than 50 sites and megasites). The tricky part is targeting the most interesting companies and then trying to identify people at companies who may be willing to talk by phone or in person about the firm's main challenges and needs and the industry's trends. Remind your aspiring careerist, this is a fact-finding mission, not yet a job search.

Fire: Getting the Right Job

NOW THAT YOUR CHILD has identified his skills and dreams and narrowed down possible careers, the next step is to start matching dreams and passions with reality. Barkley suggests that after sorting through all the information gathered from her surveying technique, your child should write a customized proposal for the most interesting companies that seem like a good match between employer and employee. The proposal should contain a compelling statement of purpose (why she is writing the proposal), list the needs she can address for the employer, outline proposed steps for solving those needs, specify what the employer will gain, describe her ability to deliver those gains, and suggest the next step and time frame.

The job search does not have to cost a lot of money. There are plenty of outfits eager to take money for their services, but encourage your kids instead to find the many free résumé-writing resources, interviewing workshops, and even career counseling, company research, and job hunting services you will find below.

Résumé

Some job seekers send out dozens, even hundreds, of résumés to every company HR department they can think of and every classified ad remotely in their desired field. Sending random résumés is an unfocused and often ineffective approach to job hunting. Career guru Richard Bolles, author of *What Color is Your Parachute?*, says that for every 1,470 résumés in circulation, only one person gets a job. The key is not quantity, but quality—of the résumé, and of the targeted employer.

Barkley believes her surveying system is much more effective than the traditional résumé and interview approach. At some point, though, potential employers are bound to request a résumé. Entry-level job seekers should create at least one résumé outlining education, any experience, and career objectives. It is wise to customize a résumé for each type job your child applies for. The résumé should highlight work and internship experience, listing most recent jobs first. Relevant courses taken and honors achieved, special skills such as computer expertise, foreign languages, or operation of relevant machines or equipment should be listed. Extracurricular activities (i.e., academic related or volunteer work, but not hobbies) indicate high motivation and the ability to juggle several things at once.

Important tips to suggest to your young résumé writer:

■ Proofread carefully. Spelling or grammatical errors are likely to knock an applicant right out of the running.

■ Be brief. Entry-level applicants should keep the résumé to one page. Be clear but succinct, and go easy on the adjectives.

■ Organize.

■ Use action-oriented verbs. For instance: oversaw, designed, implemented, managed.

■ Never ever lie. Exaggeration or creative embellishment may get a candidate an interview, but the real goal is to get and keep a good job. Once lies emerge (and they often do), it is hard to restore a tarnished reputation.

The trick to writing a stand-out résumé when your child has limited, if any, work experience is to extract skills obtained and achievements made at even the most menial, unrelated jobs. This is not intended to be an exercise in creative fiction writing. Instead, the idea is to identify transferable skills learned in previous jobs that can be applied to a desired future job. Your child needs to help potential employers make the connection between skills he has acquired from previous jobs and the skills they require in the job he wants. Susan Quattrociocchi developed *Table 6.3*, on the following page, to help job seekers identify their most marketable transferable skills.

TABLE 6.3

Your Transferable Skills

YOUR JOB	JOB YOU WANT
Food server	Receptionist

JOB DUTIES	JOB DUTIES
Seat customers	Greet people
Take food orders	Keep guest log
Serve food and drinks	Answer phones
Handle cash	Take messages
Help other servers	Refer calls to the right person

SKILLS YOU HAVE	SKILLS THEY NEED
■ Working with the public in a friendly, welcoming manner	■ Working with the public in a friendly, welcoming manner
■ The ability to handle multiple tasks at the same time	■ The ability to handle multiple tasks at the same time
■ An eye for detail that enables you to be extremely accurate and do the job right	■ An eye for detail that enables you to be extremely accurate and do the job right
■ A teamwork-oriented attitude that makes you a natural at working with others and helping coworkers	■ A teamwork-oriented attitude that makes you a natural at working with others and helping coworkers

Source: *Smart Choices! About Teen Jobs: A Guidebook for Students, Parents, Educators & Employers,* by Susan Quattrociocchi, Ph.D. (Steve Laing Communications, 1995)

About half of all mid-sized companies and most large corporations are scanning résumés into their own databanks and/or tapping into electronically submitted résumés at on-line job banks. Increasingly, so are employment agencies. Many college career centers maintain an electronic database of college students' résumés for recruiters. Job seekers can also send their résumé electronically to several sites, which employers can scan when searching for candidates. For instance, check out:

- Virtual Job Fair (www.vjf.com)
- Career Blazers (www.cblazers.com)
- CareerMosaic (www.careermosaic.com)
- JobCenter (www.jobcenter.com)
- JobTrak (www.jobtrak.com)—available only to students or alumni
- Online Career Center (www.occ.com)
- PursuitNet (www.tiac.net/users/jobs/index.html)— this site even matches your résumé and skills to related job openings in its database.

Electronic résumés require different rules than traditional résumés. You may not know whether a company scans résumés, so it pays to make sure it will grab the attention of electronic as well as human eyes. Joyce Lain Kennedy, who has published several career books, including *Electronic Résumé Revolution* (John Wiley & Sons, 1995), suggests:

- Computers search for "key words" that define criteria for each job. They will pass right by résumés that don't include such words—which tend to be nouns, such as job titles, skills, and degrees, not action verbs that work on traditional résumés. It's a good bet to include words used in a classified ad or job posting.

- The job seeker's name should be the first item on each page.

- Computers are not impressed with fancy graphics. In fact, ornamentation can confuse a computer and may never even come before the eyes of a human being. When filing a résumé to an on-line job bank, avoid underlining, italics, horizontal or vertical lines, or fancy fonts or formats.

- Avoid staples and folds (especially on lines of text).

Here are a few good résumé-writing resources:
- *From College to Career: Entry Level Résumés for Any Major,* by Donald Ascher (Ten Speed Press, 1992)
- *Your First Résumé,* by Ron Fry (Career Press, 1996)
- College career centers often provide free résumé-writing seminars and have counselors who will critique students' résumés.

Interviews

Is your child nervous at the prospect of being grilled during those first job interviews? For some, that nervousness never goes away, no matter how far they have climbed on their career ladder. This might be a great time to share with your child your own experiences at job interviews. What memories do you have about the very first job interview, or the most recent ones? What were some of the tricky questions you recall; which did you answer especially well; and which did you botch? Your stories can help your child feel you empathize and understand what they are going through, and the comic relief can take the edge off some of their anxiety.

The most important advice you can offer your children is to prepare for the interview. That not only means anticipating and practicing how they would answer questions, but also researching the company: its size, recent growth pattern, culture, competitors, products, services, and industry trends. It's easy to find information about publicly traded companies; most libraries and college career placement centers have corporate directories—such as *Standard & Poors' Register of Corporations, Directors, and Executives; The 100 Best Companies to Work for in America,* by Robert Levering and Milton Moskowitz (Plume Books, 1994); and *Dun & Bradstreet's Book of American Business* or *Dun & Bradstreet's Million Dollar Directory*—that list basic information. Many companies, even small and privately held ones, have Web sites; on-line directories and search engines such as Yahoo!, Metacrawler, Infoseek, Alta Vista, Lycos, HotBot, and Excite can identify information about many companies, as can the many on-line job search sites—some of which are listed in the Appendix. Industry trade associations, local and regional business periodicals, and chambers of commerce are other useful sources.

Interviewees should prepare to ask their own questions about the job, company, and industry—questions that will help candidates decide whether or not this job and company are a good fit. The interview is a two-way street, where interviewer and interviewee are sizing each other up. Candidates who ask intelligent questions are more impressive than those who passively answer questions thrown their way.

For practice handling typical interview questions, suggest your child check out E.span's practice interview module on-line at www.espan.com/docs/intprac.html.

There's a big difference between practicing for interviews and being in one. Encourage your kid to anticipate and think through all sorts of possible questions. But in the end, the objective is to find a good match. Matches based on pretensions and canned responses are not likely to be comfortable for employee or employer. MetLife's First Job Web site suggests other commonsense, but not always heeded, interview advice:

- Dress appropriately
- Arrive on time
- Listen to questions carefully and answer directly
- Ask questions
- Avoid talking about salary and benefits
- Offer a firm handshake at the beginning and end of the interview, and maintain eye contact during discussions
- Send a thank-you note

Other sources about preparing for job interviews:

- *Adams Job Interview Almanac: 1800 Interview Questions and Answers* (Adams Media, 1996)
- *Your First Interview,* by Ron Fry (CareerPress, 1996)

Employment Tests

Companies increasingly put job candidates through a battery of tests, to measure intelligence or skills, psychological profile, honesty, and drug or alcohol presence. If your child wants to be considered for employment at such companies, she will probably have to take whatever tests the employer requires.

Rivchun points out, "There are so many things companies can't do to separate out candidates. They can't by age, gender, or ethnicity. One of the things they can do is give you a test." Reassure your child not to be afraid of the results. "There are things employers will reward sooner than high scores on any test, such as coming across on a résumé or in an interview as really caring about the company, or demonstrating that the candidate can deliver and finish things. Applicants may find it useful to learn what strengths and weaknesses the tests indicate they have."

It's a good idea to hold off on the tests until as late in the process as possible, notes Nella Barkley. "Before you take tests, you want to be sure you're interested in the organization, and that you're well suited to work there." She says she has no problem with competency or drug tests, but considers psychological tests to be an invasion and an insult. Moreover, some psychological tests are less than reliable. The prospective employer should be willing and able to explain how the test questions relate to the requirements of the job for which the candidate is applying, and who will see the results.

If asked to take them by a company the candidate truly wants to work for, Barkley suggests, "At least make sure the complete information and feedback are given to you. I do not think it is fair nor wise to give other people information about yourself and be unaware of it."

"If you're not comfortable with a test, you may not be comfortable with that organization," points out Acker. She says that Procter & Gamble conducts aptitude tests at some point in the hiring process. Half the initial candidates don't follow through with the test. "That's okay," she says. "It's a screening device for both parties." Job seekers who are turned off by these tests would likely be uncomfortable with the culture of companies that require candidates to take employment tests. Companies that test applicants don't have to waste time and resources on prospects who are not likely to fit in with that company's culture.

There are some advantages to employment tests. To the extent the questions reveal information about the position, the candidate can learn whether the job is a good fit. Also consider that a company that tests candidates is willing to invest time and money to seek top-notch employees. Those who take them and pass them can get a much-needed ego boost in what can sometimes feel like a demoralizing job-hunting process.

Where to Search

Many of my successful job searches have resulted from informal networking. The dean of my grad school put me in touch with *Forbes* magazine's former economics editor, an alumnus of the university, who was looking for an assistant. A writer I had worked with there gave me a tip that Tom Peters was looking for a business writer/editor to launch a newsletter. An ad my mother found in the *Penny Saver* in her small New England town was the source of my last job, as senior editor of *Family Business* magazine, then based in the Berkshires. (I almost did not pursue this lead because I doubted a serious magazine would be advertised in the *Penny Saver,* but the job opened up a fascinating area of specialization for me.)

Lesson: You never know beneath what stone a great job may be hiding. Some career experts still sneer at on-line job sites, but they are proliferating, being used by more and more employers and recruiters, and becoming more sophisticated. Others scoff at classifieds because they can elicit hundreds or thousands of competing applications. Encourage your college grad to be broad-minded enough to pursue a combination of traditional and offbeat avenues, but emphasize quality over quantity. Dissuade her from dissipating her energy chasing every blip on the radar screen.

What do employers prefer? The top five recruiting methods for both 1997 and 1998, according to NACE's annual Job Outlook Survey of employers, included on-campus recruiting, career/job fairs, employee referrals, job postings to career offices, and requesting résumés from career offices. However, the Internet seems to be gaining respect among employers. In 1997, companies responding to NACE's Job Outlook Survey rated Internet job postings as 11th among preferred recruiting methods, with a 2.65 on a scale of one to five. In 1998 the Internet jumped to 6th place, with a 3.31 score—leapfrogging internship programs, recruitment advertising, faculty contacts, newspaper advertising, and student organizations and clubs.

College career centers

The NACE Job Outlook Survey provides evidence that students can find companies seriously looking to recruit through a variety of college career services, including on-campus recruiting, résumé and interview workshops, personal career counseling, career and job fairs, job postings at career offices, résumé banks, and internship and co-op programs. Computer-assisted guidance programs can help students assess their skills and interests and research occupations that suit them. Students are wise to take advantage of these services!

On-line

Surfing the net for a job can help identify job postings that cannot be found elsewhere. The problem is, there are thousands of career Web sites, and new ones pop up all the time. When I typed the word "job" in several Internet search engines, I uncovered 738,543 "matches" on Alta Vista and 1,013,101 on Excite. (My search on Lycos for "jobs" found mainly sex sites! You may have better luck searching the word "career" or "occupation.")

There are three main types of on-line employment sites: job banks, which provide searchable databases of job listings; résumé databases, where you can send your résumé electronically for recruiters to find (see earlier section in this chapter on résumés); and career-information services that offer advice in résumé writing, interviewing techniques, and information about different careers and job trends. Some "megasites" offer combinations of the above services. Check out the many on-line sites listed in the Appendix.

The Riley Guide (www.dbm.com/jobguide/multiple.html) is a great place to start.

Usenet newsgroups or listservs allow groups of people to hold on-line discussions. When subscribers post their comments and questions to the list's e-mail address, their inquiry is forwarded to all other subscribers. Job-related groups discuss issues and trends, offer each other career-related advice, and may even critique each others' résumés and cover letters. Campus libraries and career centers carry Internet directories with lists of groups in different fields. Professional journals often list on-line services as well.

Books about on-line job searches include:

- *Adams Electronic Job Search Almanac,* by Emily Ehrenstein (Adams Publishing, 1997, $9.95).

- *Electronic Résumés and On-line Networking,* by Rebecca Smith (Career Press, 1999, $13.99).

- *Hook Up, Get Hired!: The Internet Job Search Revolution,* by Joyce Lain Kennedy (John Wiley & Sons, 1995, $45.00).

- *Job Searching On-line for Dummies,* by Pam Dixon and Ray Marcy (IDG Books Worldwide, 1998, $24.99).

- *Point and Click Job Finder,* by Seth Godin (Dearborn Trade, 1996, $14.95).

- *The Quick Internet Guide to Career and College*

Information, by Anne Wolfinger (Jist Works, 1997, $9.95).

■ *Using the Internet and the World Wide Web in Your Job Search,* by Fred Edmund Jandt and Mary B. Nemnich (Jist Works, 1995, $16.95).

Networking

The majority of jobs are never advertised or listed. The best way to tap this "hidden job market" is by word of mouth among family, friends, friends of the family, professors, alumni, and previous employers. Career and job fairs sponsored by colleges are great places to expand one's network. If your child has followed Nella Barkley's surveying process of identifying industries and companies, the people your child has met with are now part of his or her network.

It pays for job seekers to let everyone know what they are looking for, to meet with anyone even remotely connected to the field, and to circulate résumés to anyone who knows anyone in an industry, company, or functional area related to your child's desired field.

Classifieds

Many ads are "blind"—they don't identify the organization, and there is no name or even department listed. It could be a department head or a personnel manager at a large or small company, or a recruiter for an employment agency. When responding, tell your kid to make sure the cover letter specifies the publication in which the ad appeared and the date and position advertised (the company or recruiter may have placed several ads in that and other newspapers for one or more job openings). Candidates should make sure their cover letter and résumé highlight any skills and types of experience they have that the ad indicates the employer is looking for. For instance, an ad in my local paper for a graphic artist required proficiency in specific software programs on the Macintosh, as well as ability to work under tight deadlines and a great sense of humor. Another ad, for a sales and marketing manager at a hotel, emphasized the need for experience in on- and off-site sales, marketing, and management of a sales and marketing department.

Employment agencies

First, you can help your child understand the difference between employment agencies and headhunters. Normally, employment agencies make matches between potential employees and employers for lower-level positions. Employment agencies may advertise for certain positions and maintain files of unsolicited résumés that job hunters send them that they match with openings. Headhunters proactively go out and recruit people for client companies, much like the NBA recruits new players. Although headhunters fill high-level positions, they also look to snap up talented college grads with majors that are in high demand, such as computer science or electrical engineering.

Both employment agencies and headhunters are paid by the client company, so they are more concerned about meeting their clients' needs than the job seekers' needs. That doesn't mean your child should avoid these services, but they should approach them with healthy skepticism. They can help your child get a feel for the job market in the desired field, learn about opportunities in other fields not previously considered, and get practice being interviewed. However, the University of Massachusetts' Acker warns job hunters to beware of fine print in an agency agreement. It's rare, but some may specify that the job seeker pay a percent of the first year's salary to the agency, or have other unpleasant terms and commitments.

When a headhunter approaches your recent or soon-to-be college grad, you can bet that your kid has very marketable skills. Headhunters/recruiters who haunt top business school campuses, for example, often wine and dine candidates and may promise five-figure sign-on bonuses and other enticing perks. This can be extremely ungrounding to a kid right out of college. Your job is to help her examine more than one or two options and scrutinize offers to make sure the headhunter isn't misrepresenting the job.

Even if your child is not hired, the experience can be helpful. Suggest that she call the headhunter to get feedback about why she didn't get the job. That can be a big help with future rounds of job hunting.

Temporary staffing services

If your college grad is having trouble identifying or finding a fast-track job, a temporary position can be a great launching pad. Even if the temp job involves just typing, it can provide exposure to different industries, companies, and departments. Undirected and undecided job seekers can narrow down choices and then pursue a more permanent position after they have had a chance to get some experience and increase the pool of people with whom to network. It's also a way to begin developing real-world job experiences to fill out that résumé.

Interim assignments often involve much more than typing and answering phones, says Bruce Steinberg, associate editor at *Staffing Industry Report* and former director of research and public relations at the National Association of Temporary and Staffing Services. "Computer programmers, accountants, attorneys, paralegals, and graphic artists can find short-term stints. It's a great way for any young professional to try to break into almost any field or company," says Steinberg. He adds that permanent job seekers who are having trouble getting a foot in the door of a company they'd like to join can call the human resources department of that organization to find out which temporary service they use. "Just tell that staffing company you want to be placed as a temp at that particular company. It may just work."

During graduate school, I was a temporary typist. It paid the rent and gave me flexibility not to work during exam weeks or major research projects. In two years, I worked at about 20 different companies, from the customer service department at an airline, to a marketing research firm, to a headhunting agency specializing in cosmetic-industry executives. I took pride in doing a good job and learning about whatever I was typing, asked my bosses lots of questions, and often read up on interesting topics to which I was exposed. By the time I finished my coursework, I had a network of executives to approach about job leads, a good idea about what to look for in a company and a job, and several offers for entry-level management positions.

Unsolicited applications

Similar to a salesperson's cold-calling, sending a résumé and cover letter to the human resources department of a company is often a shot in the dark, unless the job seeker's research has uncovered a specific opportunity. For help targeting and researching potential employers, the local library may have a copy of *The National Jobbank—Employment Guide to Over 19,000 American Companies*. It lists companies by state, contact information, common positions filled, educational background sought, job-search advice, and benefits.

Evaluating Job Offers

YOUR CHILD MAY THINK he has a picture of his dream job. But when offers start rolling in, it may be tough to evaluate the best opportunity. The more your child knows about the job, the offer, and the company, the better able he will be to make an informed decision. He may need to go back to the hiring manager or human resources contact to get more information. Remind your kids to find other employees at the company to contact. Many bosses who've made an offer will make the candidate's prospective colleagues available.

Salary is obviously an important consideration, but what other criteria belong in the equation? Some factors

NACE recommends job seekers consider include responsibility, recognition, autonomy, challenge, advancement potential, schedule, working conditions, salary, fringe benefits, training programs, location of job, commuting distance, company size, company reputation, friendliness of coworkers, and the evaluation system. Other important factors include company culture and tuition reimbursement programs.

There are no "shoulds" here. A student saddled with high college-loan repayments may need to put salary near the top of the list, while others may feel strongly about living in a certain region or having flexible hours. You can remind your kid that it's important that she prioritize the factors that are most important to her (not you or anyone else!), and that she get information from each prospective employer about each factor. It may seem obvious, but kids overwhelmed by many job offers can become too confused to do the obvious.

When comparing salaries offered by employers in different geographic areas, remember to factor in cost-of-living differences. A $30,000 starting salary in Albuquerque, New Mexico, will go much farther than the same pay in New York City. On-line salary calculators (such as www.homefair.com/homefair/cmr/salcalc.html) can tell you how much more you need to earn in a high-cost-of-living city to match the standard of living you would have earning a given salary in a city with a low cost of living.

Three key benefits are first-rate medical plans, savings plans, and retirement programs. Disability and life insurance are also important benefits, as are vacations, tuition assistance, and training.

Compare each company's health insurance copayments, employee share of premiums, choice of medical providers, dental, and optical coverage. When evaluating savings and retirement programs, focus on matching contributions, vesting period, and choice of investment vehicles. Focus mostly on benefits that will improve the quality of life today, such as premium health insurance, company day care, parental leave, and telecommuting and flex time, suggest Stephen M. Pollan and Mark Levine, authors of *Die Broke: A Radical, Four-Part Financial Plan* (HarperBusiness, 1997). They explain, "Long-term benefits, like pension plans, are worthless. Most of you will be fired long before you are fully vested."

Fortune magazine's Web site (www.pathfinder.com/fortune/1996/961223/ben.html) has gathered and rated five companies' medical, retirement, savings, and lifestyle benefits, and includes an empty column which job seekers can fill in to compare with benefits at current or prospective employers.

Resources

■ *Adventure Careers: Your Guide to Exciting Jobs, Uncom-mon Occupations and Extraordinary Experiences,* by Alexander Hiam, Susan Angle, and Alex Hiam (Career Press, 1992, $11.99).

■ *Guide to Your Career,* by Alan B. Bernstein, C.S.W., P.C. and Nicholas R. Schaffrin (Princeton Press, 1998, $21.00).

■ *Jobs in Paradise: The Definite Guide to Exotic Jobs Everywhere,* by Jeffrey Maltzman (HarperPerennial Library, 1993, $15.00).

■ *What Color is Your Parachute?,* by Richard Nelson Bolles (Ten Speed Press, 1998, $16.95).

All the information and advice presented in Chapters 1 through 5 has been leading up to this chapter. You've planted and nurtured solid roots by teaching your kids about, and helping them experiment with, economic realities such as allowance, saving, investing, budgeting, credit use, and consumption. You've helped them sprout strong wings by actively engaging them in the financial maze of getting to and through college. Finally, you are about to watch and help them leave the nest and fly on their own, empowered by your patient, determined efforts to make them financially savvy, responsible, and (gulp) independent.

I hope that along the way, this book has enhanced your own economic IQ and confidence. In Chapter 7, I attempt to demystify and defuse some touchy, uncomfortable financial hot buttons, to make it easier for you to think through and discuss with your children what may feel like taboo topics.

TABLE 6.4

Tips to Help Young Job Hunters

1. Help your child start exploring career options as early as freshman year in college.

2. Encourage your child to gain experience in and try out different types of jobs through internships, work-study co-op jobs, and summer employment. The experience will give them an edge in their future job hunt and help them rule out careers they end up not liking while there's time to switch majors.

3. Become a coach. Treat your child with the respect you would a client.

4. Don't think you know it all—or anything—when it comes to today's job market. Unless you've been pounding the pavement yourself in the last three years, expect all the rules and the job market to have changed dramatically.

5. Don't get *too* practical when your child starts considering what she wants to be and do. Dreams *are* practical; energy, enthusiasm, and passion are marketable traits.

6. Help kids who have trouble figuring out what they want to be and do by listing their interests (even those that don't seem work-related), and then brainstorming together types of jobs that suit those interests, and types of employers that would hire people to do such jobs.

7. Point your kids to their college career center, which can offer career counseling, résumé and interviewing workshops, reference material, job fairs, and other resources and programs.

8. Don't ignore manufacturing companies—they are hiring new college grads at more than twice the rate as service companies. Both are facing a shortage of qualified employees.

9. Explore creative self-employment opportunities. Grad-uates in computer consulting, graphic design, and many professions can relatively easily and inexpensively set themselves up as sole practitioners.

10. Before applying for jobs, your kids can research different industries, jobs, and companies, and find people in them to interview so they can become better informed about what needs exist "out there" that they might be able to meet, and to establish a network that can later be tapped.

11. A job search does not have to cost a lot of money. Many services, such as those offered by college career centers, are free.

12. Résumés should be customized for each job application.

13. Help your kid extract skills needed for their desired jobs from previous, seemingly unrelated work and volunteer experience.

14. Make a version of your résumé that is scannable electronically. Avoid fancy graphics, fonts, and formats, and include "key words" (nouns describing titles, skills, experience, etc.) that companies' computers might search for.

15. Impress on your kids the importance of going to interviews well informed about the company, industry, products and services, culture, and competition.

16. Help kids practice being interviewed to think through how they would answer tough questions.

17. Help your kids think up intelligent questions to ask the interviewer.

18. Take advantage of every job hunting source, including on-campus recruiting, career and job fairs, Internet job postings and résumé banks, classified ads, networking, employment agencies, and temp staffing.

19. Help kids sort out their job priorities to help them weigh future offers, including responsibility, advancement potential, schedule, salary, benefits, training, location, commute time, and company culture.

Chapter 7

Answering Sensitive,

Nosy, Touchy

Questions

AS ART LINKLETTER, AND NOW BILL COSBY, HAVE observed, kids say the darndest things. They also ask the most exasperating, nosy, touchy questions, sometimes at the most embarrassing moments. Here are some scenarios that will help prepare you for what might come out of your kids' mouthes, help you think through answers that feel right to you without stifling their healthy curiosity, and even help you lighten up a bit about the areas you find most sensitive.

How much money do you make?

Many kids wonder about this. When they are very young, they have no frame of reference for understanding a dollar figure. Even $15,000 would sound like an awful lot of money to a 5-year-old, maybe even to a 10-year-old. Cheryl, a professor of tax law, says, "At 5, my daughter doesn't know the difference between a penny and a quarter. I don't think numbers mean much to her. My guess is it would suffice to tell her we have enough and more, and that we're very lucky to be as well off as we are."

Even parents of school-age kids and teens can be uncomfortable divulging their salary. "I'd never tell my children how much," says an accountant in Long Island, New York. "I would tell my 8-year-old daughter, 'You don't have to worry about money. We have enough to buy food, shelter, camp, lessons, and other things we need and want.'"

There's no absolute wrong or right. If you're comfortable discussing dollars, it's important to set clear boundaries about keeping the information in the family. Michael, an attorney and parent of 8-year-old and newborn boys, grew up never knowing how much his parents made. "I feel that this ignorance left me ill-equipped to decide what types of income I would need to live in different styles. I explained to my older son that this was not information that I was comfortable telling other people and that I hoped he would not broadcast it to all of his friends."

Providing context will help your kids understand the dollars and cents in a realistic perspective. When my 10-year-old son popped this question to me, I sat him down with a pad, pencil, and calculator, and said, "First, let's add up what all our household expenses are. Then I'll tell you how much money I make." After he recovered from the sticker shock, he was very relieved to learn that I earned enough to pay for everything, but he was surprised there wasn't more left over.

Fran, a magician and photographer in Belchertown, Massachusetts, put his earnings in a different context for his two teens: "Since I am self-employed, the amount I make can vary, depending on a number of factors. Things like my marketing and networking will make a difference as to the amount I make. I told my kids that I try to plan as well as I can, but should I not have enough money, then I work harder to find more jobs."

Who makes more money—Mommy or Daddy?

This question provides an opportunity to talk about life decisions and trade-offs you have made, and the value of an education. If both parents have jobs, you can explain how education, years of experience, types of work, and lifestyle affect income. In one family, Ike, a psychiatrist, is the sole support of the family. He and his wife explained to Alex, their 10-year-old, that because Dad spent many years going to medical school, he makes enough money for Mom to leave her job as a real estate broker to devote more time to Alex and her artwork.

Michael explained that his job as a lawyer pays more than Mommy's job as a school counselor/social worker. He also used the question to remind his son that money is only one part of what makes their home what it is and they all contribute value to it in important ways.

What would happen if you lost your job?

More and more kids are actually experiencing this; others hear about their friends' parents being out of work. Many children worry that it could happen to their parents.

If both parents work, you can start by assuring them it's unlikely that they would both lose their jobs at the same time. "Everything would be fine," Janet, vice president of new product development at a publishing company, told her 11-year-old son. "We would still have the other person's income, and we have savings."

Seth, a single father who works as a client services manager for a security company, explained to his 9-year-old daughter, "I would look for another job. I have money saved up for this kind of emergency. There is also a system called unemployment insurance that will pay me while I look for a new job."

You can also discuss sacrifices you would all be willing to make, like eating out less frequently, postponing a fancy vacation, using coupons, and waiting for sales.

How much do you have to pay in income taxes?

This is really several questions in one. Besides the actual amount, kids may not have a clear concept of what taxes are, why and how we pay them, and how we feel about paying for them.

It's a good idea, whatever your child's age, to ask them what they think taxes are, so you can correct any misconceptions they may have and inject your own philosophy about them. You should make sure they understand that everyone is supposed to contribute a portion of what they earn—about $1 for every $3 of income—to pay for government services like schools, bridges, roads, the military, and garbage collection. Our tax dollars help people who can't afford to pay for rent, food, or medical treatments. Taxes also fund our space exploration program.

If you have a job, you can explain that your company automatically subtracts your share of taxes from your paycheck. Show them a pay stub if you're comfortable doing so. If you are self-employed, explain that business owners make payments four times a year based on what they earned in each time period. At the end of the year, taxpayers must fill out several forms adding up all the money they earned and taxes they paid. You can tell kids over 10, if they're interested, that the government allows you to deduct from your tax bill a portion of certain expenses you had for your home, business, and child care, so sometimes you may get a refund. But if it turns out you paid too little, you may owe the government more money.

Have you ever cheated on your income taxes?

Few people like paying taxes, but it is your obligation to pay your share. Seth reminds his 9-year-old daughter that not doing so would be a crime and could be punishable by jail. Roger, a stockbroker, explained to his younger children that there are consequences for cheating—for example, if they cheat on a game, they get disqualified.

"We try to avoid taxes, but we do not evade them," Dan, a pastor, told his teenage son and daughter.

Craig, a family business consultant, showed his teenagers a tax form and walked them through it, explaining that he takes as many deductions as he possibly can, including providing income for them so they can pay taxes at lower rates, but emphasized that he doesn't cheat.

How much money do you give to charity?

This is one topic you may want to bring up, whether or not your kids do. Kids may be less interested in how much you give than to whom you contribute and how you make your decisions. As discussed in Chapter 4, Shel, a writer and marketing consultant, sits down twice a year with his wife, Dina, and their 10-year-old daughter, to review all the solicitations for donations they get, which they keep in a file. Together they decide how much of their giving budget will go to which organizations.

Craig says his family makes decisions related to charitable giving. "We are significant enough charitable givers to have our name displayed around our synagogue and our daughters appreciate that. Our older daughter raises money and works at a camp that takes kids from the inner city to the mountains for a week. Part of our charitable decisions is governed by the public service activities of our children. If they're willing to make a sweat equity investment in a particular charity, we're willing to invest in that."

Many families give the 10 percent the Bible says people should tithe. "We stress that out of our income a portion— the 'first fruits'—should go to the church. The order of importance is to pay God, then pay yourself (a savings program), then pay others," says Pastor Dan.

When you die, how much money will I inherit?

We may assume kids want to know how much, down to the last cent, they are in for. But younger kids may be more focused on your neat stuff. When my son was about 8, he wanted to know if he'd get my two guitars. I told him he'd get most of everything, except for a few things I would want close friends and relatives to have.

You may also want to take advantage of your kids' morbid curiosity to discuss which relatives or close friends you've arranged for them to live with, and assure them that they would be well taken care of.

"My daughter asked me at age 8—when I told her who her guardians would be if Mommy and Daddy died. She asked if she and her brother would split the money," says one father. "I said yes, other than bequests to church."

My own tendency is to be upfront with numbers, but many parents are uncomfortable doing so. You can at least assure them that they will be well provided for, with whatever life insurance and other assets you have.

(For kids in intact families): What would happen if you two got divorced?

There are never any guarantees, but regardless of the strength of your marriage, your kids are probably less concerned about the dollars and cents than the living and visitation arrangements.

Cheryl's 5-year-old daughter hasn't thought to ask this so far, but if it were to come up, Cheryl says, "First I'd reassure her that it's very unlikely that would happen. But in the event it did, she would still have two parents who loved her very much. And financially it wouldn't change our situation in any significant way."

(For kids of divorced parents): How come I get more allowance/have fewer chores at my other parent's house?

Kids are perfectly capable, at just about any age, of understanding and accepting that different homes have different rules. The more you and your ex-spouse can coordinate, the better. More important is that you clarify your own rules and standards, and be vigilantly consistent about applying them within your home.

(For kids in blended families): How come my stepsister or stepbrother has more money than I do?

It's no one's business what kids get from their parents in different households. But they have a point if they see their stepparent giving a stepsibling under the same roof more money or privileges, unless there is a significant age difference. Stepfamilies have three to six coparents trying to blend their individual financial values and priorities to make money decisions. The only way to keep the peace is to ignore the rules in the ex-spouse's home but carefully coordinate within your own household.

If you don't have enough money to buy me stuff I want, why don't you just go to the ATM machine?

If you have a child older than 7 or 8 asking you this, then as Desi used to warn Lucy, "You got some splainin' to do." Use every trip to the bank, grocery store, and shopping mall to explain the comings and goings of money. Whenever you pay by ATM card, check, or credit card, describe the mechanics of how you end up paying for things: Explain that with an ATM card and some checking accounts, you pay a fee each time you use them, and you pay interest whenever you charge more in a month than you can repay.

As one father told his 7-year-old daughter, "ATMs don't just print money. In order to take money out of the ATM you have to put money into the bank. Even though I have money in the bank, that money has been budgeted for items such as rent, food, and clothing. It must be used for the necessities first."

Craig explained to his two teens, "What we buy is really a question of how we decide to allocate money. I've adopted a saying from one of my clients: 'You can have anything you want, but you can't have everything you want.' You have to make choices. There are trade-offs in economics and personal economics."

Why can't I give my best friend $20 from my bank if I want to? It's my money!

Kids are sometimes inspired to give overly magnanimous and perhaps inappropriate gifts to friends. They may think such a gesture would win over a friend. Parents who believe in letting children learn from their mistakes may risk putting the parents of the recipient in an awkward position. They may not allow Johnny to accept such a gift. Not permitting the gift risks dampening your child's generous spirit.

Instead of dictating whether or not you allow your child to make this gift, sit down and ask your child her purpose. Compliment her on her generous intention. Then brainstorm with your child about other ways to be a good friend, and other ways to be sharing and caring.

I don't care if I don't get allowance; I just don't want to clean my room or study for that dumb test!

If you are hearing this statement, your kid is right. As I warned in Chapter 1, coupling allowance with grades, chores, or behavior can set up power struggles. If you threaten to withhold allowance when your kids don't perform as you expect them to, you give them leverage to use that against you. They can justify not doing what you demand or expect them to do and claim not to care about allowance.

The best way to handle this is to find other consequences, related to the rules they break. For instance, if your daughter refuses to do her chores, you can refuse to do things she expects you to do for her, like drive her to soccer practice. When your son turns in a disappointing report card or test grade, you can insist on no TV or computer games until he pulls his grades back up. If he hits his sister, you can tell him he can't have any friends over until he's compensated by making her bed every day for a week. Remember, the main goal of allowance is to teach kids how to handle money. By withholding money as a punishment, you defeat that purpose.

Why can't we buy things that other families have? We have the money.

Teaching kids not to look over their shoulder and feel they need or deserve to have everything that other families have can be a tough job. It's not something you can just explain once and expect them to agree and accept. The process will be ongoing and they will test the limits you set and your mettle from time to time.

When the subject comes up in Cheryl's household, she tells her 5-year-old daughter, "We make different choices. Different families choose to spend their money in different ways. We may not have the same priorities. But we don't know how much money other families have—and that's none of our business—but these are the choices we've made."

Roger reminds his sons, "We probably have things that other people don't have and don't need. We all are different (thank God!)."

"We make decisions based on what's best for our family—we're not trying to keep up with the Joneses,"

Craig tells his teen daughters.

With any question your kids hurl your way, remember that you don't have to have all the answers, and there isn't always a universal right answer. Whenever your kids totally stump you or catch you off guard, take a deep breath and take the time to have a meaningful dialogue. Who knows? You may learn a thing or two from them!

TABLE 7.1

Tips for Dealing with Tough Questions

1. Coordinate with your spouse about how to approach sensitive questions before they arise.

2. Set clear boundaries about keeping information about family finances within the family.

3. Provide a context when kids ask how much you earn or spend.

4. Focus on maintaining consistency with your own rules and philosophies and those of your current partner's instead of trying to force alignment with an ex-spouse about using the same approach.

5. Emphasize, though, that it's important to respect and accept that different households have different rules, different financial circumstances, and different ideas.

6. Discuss how education, hard work, and lifestyle decisions affect family finances.

7. If kids are worried about money, explain how family savings, government benefits, and sacrifices you might all make in a financial setback would provide a cushion and help your family bounce back.

8. Use every trip to the bank, grocery store, and shopping mall to explain the comings and goings of money.

Appendix

On-line Resources for Becoming a Financially Savvy Family

THE INTERNET CAN BE A GREAT WAY FOR PARENTS who don't feel well versed in one financial area or another to learn together. I have compiled (and provided some highlights of) Web sites, addresses, and phone numbers when relevant, to help you and your kids learn and have fun together, whatever end of the financial literacy spectrum you are on. My selection for listing is in no way an endorsement of any products or services the Web companies may offer.

Use *Table A.1* on the following page to flag Web sites geared for your kids' age level.

TABLE A.1

Internet Ratings Guide

PG13	Parental guidance suggested
K–6	Primary schoolers
7–12	Secondary schoolers
YA	Young adults (college age and above)
P	Parents

Keep in mind that new Web sites appear and old ones disappear all the time. If you have questions regarding kids and money, please check out my new Web site, members.aol.com/MoneyKids/Index.html, where I will give regular updates on new and useful sites.

Allowance

Parent Soup Message Boards (P)

www.aol.com/parentsoup *(For AOL subscribers only)*
■ Articles, book lists for parents and children, survey results

Kids' Money (PG13, P)

www.pages.prodigy.com/kidsmoney
■ Articles
■ Lists of books, links to articles for kids and parents
■ Surveys and survey results

Banking

College Board (PG13, 7–12, YA)   *800-626-9795*

www.collegeboard.org (type "checkbook balancer" on the home page search engine)

■ Five fill-in-the-blank steps to balancing your checkbook, but doesn't have a calculator that automatically balances your account

The College Board
11911 Freedom Drive, Suite 400
Reston, VA 20910

FDIC's Learning Bank (PG13, 7–12)   *800-276-6003*

www.fdic.gov/learning/index.html

■ Describes how banks work and the role of the Federal Deposit Insurance Corp.

Sovereign Bank's KidsBank (PG13, 7–12)

www.kidsbank.com

■ Lessons about money, banks, saving, electronic funds transfer

■ Quizzes on each lesson

■ Millionaire, holiday savings, and saving up for a car calculators

■ Message board where your questions get answered the next day

Young Americans Education Foundation and Bank
(PG13, 7-12, YA)   *303-321-2954*

www.theyoungamericans.org

■ Describes the history of money

■ Calculates future cost of college tuition, how much you have to save to become a millionaire using different types of investments (savings account, bonds, mutual funds, stock market), and time horizons

- Lists money-earning ideas
- Provides information on its programs such as Young AmeriTowne, Young Entrepreneur Programs, and a classroom savings initiative

Education Foundation
311 Steele Street
Denver, CO 80206

Budgets

American Express (YA)   *800-942-AMEX*

www.americanexpress.com/student/moneypit/budget/budget.html
- Budget calculator geared for college kids helps them list typical expenses and sources of income

Merrill Lynch (PG13, 7–12, YA)

www.plan.ml.com/family/parents/action.html
- Personal Action Plan helps parents help kids make a strategy for saving up for something they want

www.plan.ml.com/family/inflation-calc.html
- Inflation Calculator lets you calculate how much a car, jeans, home, movie tickets, Caribbean cruise for two, or other items of your choice would cost in 10 to 50 years at different inflation rates

Charitable Giving

The Better Business Bureau® (PG13, 7–12, YA, P)

www.bbb.com/reports/charity.html
- Rates more than 150 charitable organizations
- Lists charitable giving criteria

Impact On-line (PG13, 7–12, YA, P)

www.impactonline.org

■ Matches volunteers with nonprofit organizations, including virtual volunteering—activities you can do from the Internet such as technical assistance (on-line research, translating material into another language for a nonprofit agency), direct contact via e-mail, or a chat room (to electronically visit a homebound person, provide on-line mentoring, help students with homework)

Internet Nonprofit Center (PG13, 7–12, YA, P)

www.nonprofits.org/

■ Library of publications and data about nonprofit organizations

■ Nonprofit locator to help find any charity in the U.S.

■ Chat room and bulletin boards

The National Charities Information Bureau (PG13, 7–12, YA, P)   *212-929-6300*

www.give.org/

■ Quick reference guide to how well 400 national charities meet its philanthropic standards

■ Tips for wise giving, and on-line ordering of full reports on the charities it evaluates (the first is free, additional reports are $3.50 each)

NCIB
19 Union Square West
New York, NY 10003

Who Cares (PG13, 7–12, YA, P)

www.whocares.org/

■ Publishes a national quarterly journal devoted to community service and social activism, challenging readers to consider new ways of fixing society's problems. Get a free full-year trial subscription by calling 800-628-1692.

College

Brigham Young University (7–12, YA, P)

801-378-INFO

ar.byu.edu/financialpath

- Exposes students to exercises that include estimating education costs, financial resources, financial aid, expected future income, borrowing costs
  Brigham Young University
  Provo, UT 84602

CampusTours (7–12, YA, P)

www.campustours.com

- Links to hundreds of on-line tours developed by colleges and universities (usually still images with text, but more and more video and audio tours are appearing)

College Board (7–12, YA, P)

www.collegeboard.com
www.collegeboard.com/html/calculator000.html

- Helps you calculate how much you should expect to contribute (called expected family contribution or EFC), how much you need to save to do so, and how repayment of student loans can impact your own and your children's future finances

- List of estimated starting incomes for college graduates in various fields

www.collegeboard.com/toc/html/tocstudents000.html

- Choosing a college: college search, college applications on-line, finding a college that fits, what admissions officers look for in students, guide to campus visits, exploring college locations
- Paying for college: college costs, financial aid, bor-

rowing for college, financial aid calculators, scholarship search, scholarships for service

CollegeNET (7–12, YA, P)

www.collegenet.com/
- Info about individual colleges and universities
- Scholarship search
- Financial aid info
- Standout program: for $9, fill out a profile that CollegeNet sends to recruiters and admissions directors, which they use to identify top college candidates

CollegeScape (7–12, YA, P)

www.collegescape.com/
- On-line college application system
- Award letter comparison worksheet
- College budget worksheet
- Monthly college loan payment calculator
- College loan repayment savings calculator

Collegiate Choice Walking Tours (7–12, YA, P)

www.collegiatechoice.com
- One- to two-hour unedited video tours (made by guidance counselors, not professional videographers) of more than 300 colleges and universities in the U.S., Canada, England, Ireland, and Scotland ($15 plus shipping each)
- Tips on making campus visits on your own
- Magazine ratings of best colleges

fastWEB (7–12, YA, P)

www.fastweb.com
- Lists information about more than 400,000 scholarships (500 awards are added or updated each day)
- Free scholarship search
- Information about student loans, work study, and grant programs

Fidelity Investments (7–12, YA, P)   *800-544-6666*

www.personal11.fidelity.com/toolbox/college/cal-
culator.html
- Calculator for figuring out future college costs

Fidelity Investments
2300 Litton Lane
Mail Zone KH1A
Hebron, KY 41048

FinAid (7–12, YA, P)
www.finaid.org
- Lists financial aid scams
- Free scholarship search
- Financial aid calculators
- Prepaid state tuition plans—terms and contact information

Free Application for Federal Student Aid (FAFSA)
800-4-FED-AID

U.S. Department of Education (7–12, YA, P)
www.fafsa.ed.gov
- Lets you complete and submit FAFSA application

Nellie Mae (7–12, YA, P)
www.nelliemae.org
- Describes repayment options
- Interactive debt counseling with calculators and work sheets

Peterson's (7–12, YA, P)   *609-243-9111*
www.petersons.com
- Data about colleges and universities
- Information about internships, financial aid, study-abroad programs, summer programs, career guidance

Peterson's
202 Carnegie Center
Princeton, NJ 08542

Princeton Review (7–12, YA, P)   *609-683-0082*

www.review.com/
■ Data about colleges and universities, with a strong antiranking stand
■ Information about financial aid, internships, summer programs, study abroad, and career guidance
Princeton Review
252 Nassau Street
Princeton, NJ 08542

Sallie Mae's Online Scholarship Service (7–12, YA, P)

www.scholarships.salliemae.com/
■ Free Online Scholarship Service via CASHE® (College Aid Sources for Higher Education), a database of scholarships, fellowships, grants, work study, loan programs, tuition waivers, internships, competitions, and work co-operative programs
■ Financial aid facts
■ Searchable database of low-cost lenders
■ College planning calculators can be used live on the Internet, or you can download CollegeCalc software and use the calculators and key information off-line
■ Calculators for forecasting college costs, savings, expected family contribution, borrowing needs, accrued interest on your loan, monthly budget, repayment estimates

Student Contests (K–6, 7–12, P)

www.studentcontests.com
■ Searchable database of contests in 33 categories
Student Contest News
P.O. Box 4314
Tulsa, OK 74159-0314

U.S. Department of Education (7–12, YA, P)
800-USA-LEARN

www.ed.gov/pubs/parents.html
- How to get ready for school early
- College cost charts
- Financial aid info

www.ed.gov/pubs/prepare/pt3.html
- Questions and activities to help you choose the right college

www.ed.gov/prog_info/SFA/StudentGuide/1997-8/index.html
- Info on parent and student loans, grants, work study, and repayment
U.S. Department of Education
600 Independence Ave. SW
Washington, DC 20202-0498

U.S. News & World Report (7–12, YA, P)
800-836-6397 ext. 1400

www.usnews.com/usnews/edu/
- Ranks colleges
- Searchable college directory outlining admissions, academics, financial aid, campus life, and international students
- Ranks financial aid best values
- Provides financial aid counselors on-line

Yahoo! (7–12, YA, P)

www.yahoo.com/Education/higher_education/
- Lists Web sites of colleges and universities
- Information and advice on academic competitions, admissions, books, distance learning, graduate education, guidance, honors programs, and lecture note-taking services

Consumer Issues

The Better Business Bureau® (PG13, 7–12, YA, P)
703-276-0100

www.bbb.com/advertising/childad.html
- Information about advertising and your child

Council of Better Business Bureaus, Inc.
4200 Wilson Blvd., Suite 800
Arlington, VA 22203-1804

FrugalFun (YA, P) *800-683-WORD*

www.frugalfun.com
- Free money-saving advice

National Institute for Consumer Education (NICE) (7–12, YA, P)

www.emich.edu/public/coe/nice/compare.html
- Comparison Shopping: How to Choose (Decision Grid)

National Institute for Consumer Education
Eastern Michigan University
207 Rackham Building
Ypsilanti, MI 48197

Credit Cards

Bank Rate Monitor (YA, P)

www.bankrate.com/brm/rate/bank_home.asp
- Banking news, advice on shopping for the best rates, latest trends in bank fees, mortgages, credit cards, home-equity loans and lines, auto loans, personal loans, and CDs

CardTrak (YA, P)

www.ramresearch.com/cardtrak/surveys/secured.
html
- Cardtrak Monthly surveys on low-rate credit cards and secured cards

Debt Counselors of America® (YA, P)   800-680-3328

www.dca.org or getoutofdebt.org/
- Chat room hosted by certified financial planners, attorneys, and counselors to address questions about debt and personal finance
- List of publications about managing credit, avoiding scams, etc. (some free, some not) and ordering info

Debtors Anonymous® (YA, P)   781-453-2743

www.debtorsanonymous.org
- Description and history of the nonprofit self-help 12-step program
- How to order its literature, audiotape, and newsletter
- How to register for groups
Debtor's Anonymous
General Service Office
P.O. Box 888
Needham, MA 02492-0009

Equifax Consumer Center (YA, P)   800-997-2493

www.equifax.com/consumer/index.html
- On-line ordering of your credit report

Experian (YA, P)   888-397-3742

www.experian.com/personal.html
- Ordering info of your credit report (free if you have been denied credit, are unemployed, a victim of fraud, on welfare, or live in Colorado, Georgia, Massachusetts,

Maryland, New Jersey, or Vermont)
- Ask Max—credit advice
- Info about credit reports, and how to get and repair credit

Experian National Consumer Assistance Center
P.O. Box 949
Allen, TX 75013-0949

The Federal Reserve Board (YA, P)   *202-452-3245*

www.bog.frb.fed.us/pubs/shop
- Lists of credit cards with low-rates
- How to calculate finance charges
- Definitions of terms

National Foundation for Consumer Credit (YA, P)
800-388-2227

www.nfcc.org
- On-line debt test to see if you are heading for trouble
- Info about credit reports, bankruptcy, and getting out of trouble

National Foundation for Consumer Credit
8611 Second Avenue
Suite 100
Silver Spring, MD 20910

National Institute for Consumer Education (NICE)
(7–12, YA, P)

www.emich.edu/public/coe/nice/facts1.html
- Articles about using credit cards wisely, avoiding fraud, evaluating incentives

Pitfalls (YA,P)   *303-771-2748*

www.pitfalls.com
- Q&A about credit, the myths of crediholics and credit doctors, and the benefits of taking responsibility

Pitfalls
P.O. Box 371613
Denver, CO 80237

United College Marketing Services (YA, P)

800-357-9009

www.collegevisa.com
- Top 10 credit tips
- On-line credit strategy seminar for college students
- Order free (for college students) transaction recorders
United College Marketing Services
2021 Midwest Road, 3rd Floor
Oak Brook, IL 60521

Entrepreneurship

Junior Achievement (PG13, 7–12, YA, P)

www.ja.org
- Description of K–12 programs, how to get involved, list of offices

LavaMind's Learning Series (PG13, 7–12, YA, P)

www.lavamind.com/edu.html
- Description and order info for games such as Gazillionaire, Zapitalism, and Profitania
- Download free shareware version of Gazillionaire

The Lemonade Stand (PG13, 7–12)

www.littlejason.com/lemonade/lemonadeb.cgi
- Simulates a lemonade stand on a neighbor's yard (for $0.75 a day rent). Based on a daily weather forecast, players must decide how many cups of lemonade to make, how much to charge, and whether to advertise. For each day's play, the game calculates how many cups you sell, your expenses that day, and your profit.

Investing

A.G. Edwards Big Money Adventure (PG13, 7–12, YA)

www.agedwards.com/bma/index.shtml

■ Rainbow Castle: games and a variety of pictures to print and color (for ages 2 to 6)

■ Storybook Adventures: lets you choose the paths the characters travel to determine how the story ends while learning about money (for ages 6 to 10)

■ Star Traders: stock-picking game where winners are awarded prizes (for ages 10 to adult)

FinanceCenter (Quicken) (PG13, 7–12, YA, P)

www.networth.galt.com

■ Directory of mutual funds for past year's top 25 best funds in 45 categories

■ Charts year-to-date prices of mutual funds

■ Lets you track your investments in up to 10 personal portfolios

■ Provides the latest news about your favorite companies

Good Money (PG13, 7–12, YA, P)

www.goodmoney.com

■ Performance of 30 Good Money Stock Average versus the Dow Jones Industrial Average

■ Social funds and banks

■ Company profiles, articles, studies, and how-to guides

■ On-line forums and chats

GreenMoney On-Line Guide (PG13, 7–12, YA, P)
800-318-5725

www.greenmoney.com
■ Links to socially responsible products, mutual funds, banks, and credit unions
■ Articles about socially responsible investing

Investing for Kids (7–12, YA, P)

www.library.advanced.org/3096
■ ThinkQuest stock market game
■ Financial quiz
■ Stock learning center
■ Goal calculator
■ Glossary of terms

invest-o-rama! (7–12, YA, P)

www.investorama.com
■ List of on-line investment clubs
■ Links to a directory of more than 7,500 investment sites in 80 categories
■ A directory of more than 4,500 public companies with Web sites

MainXchange, Inc. (7–12, YA)

www.mainxchange.com/site/sneak4/sneak4.html
■ Investment contests where teens can earn serious prizes (such as leather jackets, airline tickets, musical instruments)

The Sage Group (PG13, 7–12, YA, P) 972-818-3900

www.sage.com
■ Information on mutual funds
■ Kids Corner (on AOL only, at keyword "sage")

■ Provides articles, advice, and chat rooms

Sage US, Inc.

17950 Preston Road

Suite 800

Dallas, TX 75252

Securities Industry Foundation for Economic Education (school classes)

www.smg2000.org

■ Stock Market Game: allows classes, grades 4–12, to sign up to simulate stockmarket trading

Smith Barney Young Investors Network
(PG13, 7–12, YA)

www.smithbarney.com/yin

■ Setting savings and investment goals

■ Selecting investments to fit your goals

■ Tracking investment performance

■ Creating a cyberportfolio

■ Savings and budget, investment, and college cost calculators

Stein Roe's Young Investor Fund
(PG13, 7–12, YA, P)   *800-338-2550*

www.younginvestor.com

■ Stock market game

■ Game room with memory and trivia games, brain teasers, crosswords, and rebus puzzles (using pictures and words to make another word or phrase)

■ Information about the Young Investor mutual fund

■ Kid-to-kid surveys of investment questions and answers

Job Hunting

CareerGoal (YA, P)

www.careergoal.com/html/interviewing_101.html
- Interviewing tips
- Custom job search
- Résumé service

CareerMosaic (YA, P)

www.careermosaic.com
- Jobs database of thousands of searchable and available opportunities
- Full-text search of jobs listed in regional and occupational newsgroups
- Profiles of hundreds of world-class employers
- Post or update your résumé for free—employers come and search the database to recruit new talent
- On-line job fairs
- Tips on job hunting, résumé writing, wage and salary information
- CollegeConnection—job opportunities and entry-level resources for members of the emerging workforce

E.span (YA, P)

www.espan.com/
- Searchable job database
- Post/edit your résumé
- Employer listings
- Career library

www.espan.com/docs/intprac.html
- Practice interview module gives a series of possible answers to typical interview questions and explains why the answers you select are right or wrong

Fortune Magazine On-line (YA, P)

www.pathfinder.com/fortune/1996/961223/ben.html

- Lets you compare a potential employer's medical, retirement, savings, and lifestyle benefits to those of other companies

JobCenter (YA, P)

www.jobcenter.com
- Submit your résumé for $5 for six months
- Search job listings for free

JobHunt (YA, P)

www.job-hunt.org
- Lists and ratings of career sites
- Lists job openings, mostly in science, engineering, and medicine
- Directory of recruiting agencies

JobSmart (YA, P)

www.jobsmart.org
- Job listings in California only
- Résumé preparation tips
- On-line career guides and databanks

jobsmart.org/tools/resume/index.htm
- Tips for putting a résumé on the Internet

JobTRAK (YA)

www.jobtrak.com
- Available only to students or alumni
- Posts 3,000 new job openings daily, targeted to students and alumni

- Résumé posting
- InterviewTrak: Campus Interview System: A new service allows you to see who is recruiting on campus, submit your résumé, and sign up for interviews, all on-line
  - Job-search tips including advice on creating a résumé and negotiating a salary package, and city salary comparisons
  - Career contact database of alumni, employers, parents, and friends representing diverse career fields nationwide, who have shared their career experiences with students and alumni
  - Career Forums offer advice from career center professionals, human resources staff, and peers
  - Career Index describes thousands of careers, including the outlook in their particular industry and salary ranges
  - Personality test

The Monster Board (YA, P)

www.monster.com
- Search more than 50,000 jobs worldwide
- On-line seminars on recruitment
- Career fairs
- Info on entry-level jobs, relocation, and apartments
- Résumé builder

Online Career Center (YA, P)

www.occ.com
- One of the first Internet job sites, OCC collects résumés for its subscribers (employers)
- Provides direct links to employers seeking applicants

PursuitNet (YA, P)

www.tiac.net/users/jobs/index.html
- Matches your résumé and skills to its database of professional, technical, sales, and management job openings in the $30,000 to $100,000 salary range

Real World Internships (YA,P)   *516-295-5373*

www.reinterns.com
■ On-line applications for internships in the New York metro area (cost is $200 if you are placed)

Resumix (YA, P)

www.resumix.com/resume/resumeindex.html
■ Step-by-step guide to create, format, and submit a résumé on-line, to be compatible with the latest human resources software systems

The Riley Guide (YA, P)

www.dbm.com/jobguide
■ Job listings and industry resources on-line
■ General recruiters and location/population-specific resources
■ Find local work opportunities mostly from state employment services and newspapers
■ International job opportunities
■ Resources for women, minorities, and other groups
■ Short comments on more than 50 on-line résumé databases, and links to information for writing résumés
■ Self-employment ideas, summer work, volunteer opportunities
■ Resources for specific occupational areas
■ Career guides, salary information, info on how to research employers
■ Information on trends in employment and industry
■ Resources for targeting employers and researching an employer once you have an interview scheduled
■ Salary guides and other compensation and wage information
■ Preparing your résumé for the Internet
■ Using the Internet in your job search
■ Help with cover letters, résumés, interviews

Summer Jobs (7–12, YA, P)

www.summerjobs.com
- Search for seasonal and part-time jobs by location or keyword
- Success stories
- Links to other employment sites

Virtual Job Fair (YA, P)

www.vjf.com/faq.html
- On-line résumé posting/searching
- Listing of 20,000 high-tech career opportunities
- *High Technology Careers* magazine

What Color Is Your Parachute (YA, P)

www.washingtonpost.com/parachute
- Advice on creating and posting résumés, networking, and researching jobs
- Links to on-line job-hunting sources

World Wide Web Employment Office (YA, P)

www.harbornet.com/biz/office/annex.html
- Lists résumé sites by field or occupation
- Allows you to link your résumé to its site for $10 a year

Saving

First Technology Bank (PG13, 7–12, YA, P)

www.1sttech.com/kidsclb/kidscalc.html
- Kid's Club Savings Calculator shows how long it will take to save for various things at different weekly saving amounts

Kids' Money (PG13, 7–12, YA, P)

pages.prodigy.com/kidsmoney/
- Links to savings games, articles, resources

pages.prodigy.com/kidsmoney/piggy.htm
- Kids send in pictures of themselves with their banks

Merrill Lynch Parents' Plan (PG13, 7–12, YA, P)

www.plan.ml.com/family/parents/teach.html
- Age-specific advice on teaching kids to save

www.plan.ml.com/family/parents.save.html
- Family Saving Activity Sheet helps family members figure out how to save money by completing chores themselves instead of paying someone else

www.plan.ml.com/family/kids/index.html
- Tips from kids for saving
- Order free on-line comic book, "Time to Save"

Save for America (P)   206-746-0331

www.ed.gov/pubs/EPTW/eptw8/eptw8i.html
- Information about a computerized school savings program, run by adult volunteers, that teaches students in grades 4–6 how to maintain a savings account. Schools must be sponsored by a bank.

Save for America
4095 173rd Place SE
Bellevue, WA 98008

Miscellaneous

Council on Compulsive Gambling of New Jersey
(7–12, YA, P)   *800-GAMBLER*

www.800gambler.org
- Studies, statistics
- 20 questions to test if you have a gambling problem
- Links to more than 275 self-help Web sites
- Hotline numbers and Web sites of 36 regional affiliate offices

Shoplifters Anonymous (7–12, YA, P)   *888-466-2299*

www.shopliftersanonymous.org
- Articles about why shoplifters steal and legal consequences
- How to change behavior through education
- Quotes from shoplifters
- Information about Shoplifters Alternative—a research and rehabilitation program through home education

Shoplifters Anonymous
380 North Broadway
Jericho, NY 11753

Permissions credits

Grateful acknowledgment is made to the following publishers and organizations for permission to reproduce copyrighted material. This page constitutes a continuation of the copyright page.

For Table 1.1, "The Pros and Cons of Giving an Allowance," Source: Sharon M. Danes, Ph.D., associate professor, Minnesota Extension Service, University of Minnesota.

For Table 1.2, "Two-Tiered Allowance," Family Rules, © by Kenneth Kaye.

For Table 2.1, "The Making of a Millionaire," © Liberty Securities Corporation.

For data used in Table 2.2, "The Power of Doubling a Penny," © Liberty Young Investor Parent's Guide.

For Table 2.4, "Features of Bank Accounts," from "Making Sense of Savings," by the Board of Governors of the Federal Reserve System.

For data used in Table 2.7, "Drips With Kiddie Appeal," © The Moneypaper Guide to Dividend Retirement Plans (Temper the Times Communications, Inc.).

For data in Exercise 3.1, "How Much Credit Can Your Kid Afford?," © Fact Sheet, National Institute for Consumer Education, Eastern Michigan University.

For data used in Tables 3.1 and 3.2, "Hypothetical Income of a Typical 12-Year Old," and "Tracking a Month's Expenses," © Adapted from material prepared by Lynn White, professor and Extension family economics specialist, the Texas Agricultural Extension Service of the Texas A&M University System.

For Exercise 4.1, "Product Test Summary Sheet" and accompanying steps, © Virginia A. Atwood (1985). Bubble-good data: Product Testing and other sources.

Social Education, 49 (2), 146-149.

For Table 4.1, "Too Much Too Soon?", Nickelodeon/Yankelovich Youth MONITOR™ survey.

For Exercise 4.2, "Decision Grid," and accompanying steps, © National Institute for Consumer Education, Eastern Michigan University.

For Table 4.2, "Who Steals What, When?", by the National Retail Security Survey, conducted by Loss Prevention Specialist, Winter Park, Florida.

For Table 5.2, "Required Monthly Payment to Fund $1,000" with data provided by Robert Ortalda, C.P.A.

For Table 5.3, "Estimated Starting Incomes of College Graduates," reproduced with permission from College Board Online and Educational Testing Service Copyright © 1998 by College Entrance Examination Board. All rights reserved.

For Table 5.4, "Repayment Options for Federal Family Education Loans," © Nellie Mae.

For Illustration 6.1, "Job Circles," and Table 6.3, "Your Transferable Skills," adapted from *Smart Choices! About Teen Jobs: A Guidebook for Students, Parents, Educators, & Employers* © by Susan Quattrociocchi, Ph.D. (Steve Laing Communications, 1995).

For Table 6.2, "Classes Worth Their Weight in Gold," reprinted with permission from *Major in Success,* © by Patrick Combs, Ten Speed Press, Berkeley, California.

For material on Direct Investing quoted on pages 58–59, from *Better Investing,* August 1994, by Joan Morrissey.

For Table 6.1, "Top Ten Jobs for People Who . . .," from *Guide to Your Career,* by Alan B. Bernstein, C.S.W., P.C. and Nicholas R. Schaffrin (Princeton Review, 1998).

Index

Note: Italicized page numbers refer to tables.

About Bloomberg

Bloomberg L.P., founded in 1981, is a global information services, news, and media company. Headquartered in New York, the company has nine sales offices, two data centers, and 80 news bureaus worldwide.

Bloomberg Financial Markets, serving customers in 100 countries around the world, holds a unique position within the financial services industry by providing an unparalleled combination of news, information, and analytic tools in a single package known as the Bloomberg® service. Corporations, banks, money management firms, financial exchanges, insurance companies, and many other entities and organizations rely on Bloomberg as their primary source of information.

Bloomberg News℠, founded in 1990, offers worldwide coverage of economies, companies, industries, governments, financial markets, politics, and sports. The news service is the main content provider for Bloomberg's broadcast media, which include Bloomberg Television®—the 24-hour cable television network available in 10 languages worldwide—and Bloomberg News Radio™—an international radio network anchored by flagship station Bloomberg News Radio AM 1130℠ in New York.

In addition to the Bloomberg Press® line of books, Bloomberg publishes Bloomberg® Magazine and Bloomberg Personal Finance™.

To learn more about Bloomberg, call a sales representative at:

Frankfurt:	49-69-920-410	San Francisco:	1-415-912-2960
Hong Kong:	852-977-6000	São Paulo:	5511-3048-4500
London:	44-171-330-7500	Singapore:	65-438-8585
New York:	1-212-318-2000	Sydney:	61-29-777-8686
Princeton:	1-609-279-3000	Tokyo:	81-3-3201-8900

About the Author

Jayne A. Pearl has been a business reporter and editor for almost 20 years. She worked for *Forbes* magazine, co-launched *Family Business* magazine, and has written extensively on corporate finance, family business, and economics. Her e-mail address is MoneyKids@aol.com.